Ciffy's
Tale

Christopher A R Jauncey

DEDICATION

For Peggy...

CONTENTS

ACKNOWLEDGMENTS

I would like to thank my wife, family and friends, who have stood by me tirelessly over the years, I can never repay their love, strength, courage and unfailing loyalty, without whom I would have been truly lost forever, and everyone who did not laugh at me when I expressed the desire to write a book.

"Keep away from people who try to belittle your ambitions. Small people always do that, but the really great make you feel that you, too, can become great" - Mark Twain.

1 EARLY LIFE AND FRED THE CROW

I was born and lived in a modest first floor flat on vicarage road, this was the first home I knew, my earliest memory was as a baby believe it or not I'm told this is not possible? well to those people I say bullocks!, I can still to this very day remember holding my dad's hand through the bars of my cot with him singing to me to sleep with his rendition of the umbrella man, which my mom told me in later years mostly resulted with my dad nodding off and me sitting there laughing and chuckling wondering what was going on, with no intention of sleep, right there and then I think my life was destined to be lived on my own terms.

At the end of our long road, in King's Heath was a row of shops where mom would buy the groceries we needed, one day she took me as usual in my pram, parked me up outside the butchers, went inside to buy sausages or something, came out, promptly caught the bus home and realised she had forgot something, yes me, in a blind panic she hurried back to find me still parked outside the butchers exactly where she had left me, we always joked that they would have brought me back anyway, many years later I was to become friends with a chap who fixed my computer, it turned out that his mum and dad owned and ran that butchers shop, what a small world we live in.

As I grew in the small world of that tiny first floor flat, I managed to get myself in all kinds of daredevil scrapes, by this time I was crawling, on one occasion I can remember my mom scrubbing the stairs that lead from the sitting room down to our own front door, we had no carpet on the stairs it was something like a green plastic like linoleum with some kind of grip pattern molded into it was to be of no use whatsoever to what unfolded next, apparently I had escaped from the playpen which mom had placed me whilst she set about the task of scrubbing those slippery green plastic covered stairs and crawled my way to the top pausing momentarily to chuckle drawing her attention just before the ba-bum ba-bum!!, as I began my descent of the stairs on my front, head first like some kind of infant Olympic luge competitor, to this day I have always wanted to do the cresta run in St Moritz who says our childhood doesn't shape our future?, my mother was horrified and could only watch as I made my way down to her, luckily I was un-scathed but not a tear was shed on my part, but mom was beside herself thinking what could have happened.

The flat itself by today's standards was not very well insulated from the cold, the winters were bitter, mom tried her best to keep the flat warm with the tiny coal fire in the sitting room, I used to love to wake to see what patterns the ice had formed on the inside of the bedroom window which I had to share still with mom and dad. As a toddler this was fine but a move was certainly on the cards in a few years, as my brother was 13 years older than me he had the luxury of a bedroom to himself, I can remember vaguely one Sunday morning something happening which I must admit causes me great amusement these days, in the ground floor flat below us lived an old lady with her shall we say her unsociable son, he was in his early 20's and would delight in playing, well attempting to anyway play the old upright piano in her siting room directly below us, at the most un godly hours, one day dad snapped, he had finished a night shift and was in bed trying to sleep when it started plink plonk a plinky plonk plonk, he got up apparently only wearing his trousers and string vest went down to the coal shed, picked up the old fireman's Axe he used to break up the coal with, brought it upstairs and and banged it down several times on the wooden floor boards, later we found out showering the uncouth young adult, I use the term "Adult" loosely, with plaster from the ceiling above, we never heard the piano again thank god.

As I grew I used to play out in the tiny shared garden at the back and began to be fascinated by the creatures that lived around me, mainly in the summer as toddler I wandered the back garden which seemed as huge as a jungle I found snails, newts ant nests to play with, as I remember the garden was very un-kemped so was only allowed in there supervised on warm summer days, I can remember one day mom hanging out washing and screaming dancing from foot to foot, snake" it's a snake, it's a snake, by the time I had got anywhere near where all the action was it had long gone, my brother informed us it was a grass snake, and too this day I have still never seen one in the wild.

At around this time we were making regular weekend visits to my mom's brothers home in Cambridge, "Uncle Ken" deserves a chapter all to himself, he was a character indeed and looking back a bit eccentric too, He always had something interesting to show us, he once had a what looked like an ordinary walking stick, in fact it was a .410 shotgun that you screwed a trigger into and it held one cartridge so you could whip it out at a moment's notice and shoot a pheasant as he used to say, and another occasion he had a walking stick that he told me was made from a Brussels sprout stalk, but it looked like and felt like wood!, I never quite know if he was having me on, anyway we would set off in whatever car my dad was currently driving, and normally arrive late on a Saturday evening, Aunt Evelyn would feed us and we would all sit and talk till bedtime, where two comfy armchairs would be pushed facing together, making me a lovely cozy comfy bed, which I had no problem going to sleep on, in fact my mom used to say to me I could go to sleep on a washing line, which I did try once and failed miserably.

I would awake on Sunday morning to the smell of bacon and eggs coming from the kitchen, I would toddle in to see Aunt Evelyn busy cooking for all the family, she was as I remember a lovely woman, kind very generous not a bad bone in her whole body and always had a smile on her face that seemed to stretch ear to ear when she saw me, we would sit and eat breakfast altogether on various stools and chairs at different heights around the table, and it always seemed as if the bigger people sat on the tall stools and the littlest of us would sit on the lowest seat, with my nose barely above the table I would tuck into my breakfast looking up at my cousin, Paul perched on the tallest stool, reaching down precariously to try and eat, which used to make me giggle but one sharp glance from Uncle Ken was enough to Clam my mouth tight shut and return my glance to the table listening to the radio that always seemed to play on a Sunday all day long, after breakfast mom would help Aunt Evelyn wash up my dad would sit in the front room chatting with uncle Ken, and my cousins would go back to their rooms to listen to music, I would like to visit my cousin Paul's room as it was full of stuffed animals in glass cases, he was a proper countryman and used to shoot, fish, hunt and would always sit and tell me about any rabbits he had caught and fish it was so fascinating we would sit for hours listening to his country exploits.

At Sunday lunchtime it was traditional for the men to go to the pub whilst the Sunday roast was being cooked, Aunt Evelyn was a good cook and I loved her Sunday dinners, no trimming was spared, and I loved it, the trip to the pub was really for the men to go and swap what they had caught, grown etc and you get to trade anything in there, my dad said they would come back with veg, rabbits, hares, pheasant and my all-time favourite asparagus tips. I only found out quite recently from my Cousin Paul's son, that uncle Ken would drive down the fen early on a Sunday morning fill the boot of his car with veg, fruit, potatoes or anything he could "coax" into the boot of his car, and this is what he would trade down the pub on a Sunday lunch, he was a window cleaner by trade, but I'm not sure how much window cleaning got done, when we all used to sit down to Sunday lunch on the same various perches as breakfast the children were expected to be silent, eat their meal and asked to be excused from the table, I used to take great delight in waiting for pudding as Aunt Evelyn would always make a homemade apple pie and custard, all very simple you might think?, oh no, uncle Ken had a "thing" about custard, it had to be thick enough that you could stand your spoon up in it, we would all sit there and watch him insert his desert spoon into the custard in an upright position, and if the thickness of the custard did not support the spoon, well you would have thought Hitler had invaded England, he would say " Oh Ev, look at this bloody custard" dear me, I would giggle and titter and get the death stare from uncle Ken, which would cause him to moan even more, this isn't custard Ev?" he would go on and on, he would moan about it for the rest of the day, almost until it was time for the long drive home, we would normally then go into the back garden where the men would have a few beers and us cousins would play happily in the garden until it was time to head home in the early evening, I can always remember the pink metal garden gate at the bottom of the front path, it was the first thing and last thing I saw as we arrived and left, I remember those happy times fondly even to this day, we would normally arrive home late in the evening with me falling asleep on the back seat, the trip took quite a few hours as there were no motorways in those early days, well at least non cross country from the midlands to the fens, pyjamas on I would snuggle down into bed and think about the lovely time I had.

Soon after this we would move to a three bedroom flat as I was growing and it was important for me to have my own room, we finally moved to another first floor flat in Kingshurst, at the top of a tiny rise looking down over a field with the river Cole at the bottom, my room was next to the sitting room and had a window overlooking a small balcony, and yes, in the winter the ice still used to form wondrous patterns on the inside of the glass. I started a new school that was a fair walk and lay behind some shops which I believe are still there to this day, my mom would walk me to school in the mornings and sometimes I was allowed to go into the local shop and choose a biscuit to go with my lunch, for break time, I loved the little bedroom that overlooked the balcony, in the winter I would love to sneak out of bed and look out the window and watch the snow swirl and dance around the lamppost that lay opposite, winter nights in the 60's seemed colder longer and somehow more still, to me the world seemed to be at peace with itself, as if everyone in the world was happy quiet and still, being next to the lounge I could hear the sounds of the television as they drifted into my room, my mum and dad loved to watch drama shows in the evening, and I can remember pulling the covers tightly over my head when I heard the theme tune to "The Invaders", a Quinn Martin production the American accent bellowed out I would quake and try and listen to what the storyline was, but was never allowed to watch it as it was "totally unsuitable" for my age, when I think how things have changed these days and children of my age now happily shoot things and people to pieces in these video game consoles, makes me wonder what we've lost over the years. A TV program I was allowed to watch was the Undersea World of Jacques Cousteau as he travelled the oceans in his boat the Calypso, I absolutely loved to watch that show and many years later was instrumental in me taking up the sport of free diving, I would sit at my mums feet next to the roaring coal fire watching as this magical world unfolded before my eyes, and was so sad when it finished as I knew this signalled bedtime and I would do anything to stay up and watch TV a little longer, "mum"!! , can I have some hot milk please, as I knew this would give me the longest time to stay up, a walk to the kitchen milk warmed up in a saucepan and then sipped to death to make it last, when finally I hit the bed sheets I would pretend to be Jacques Cousteau, with my head above the sheets and of course the surface of the sea, I would take a deep breath and turn head to heels and scramble under the covers to the foot of the bed, or "sea bed" I would pretend to marvel at the different species of fish, and just before the need to breath I would head back up to the surface again, gulping for air, I would repeat this several times until I completely wore myself out and fell to sleep, I'm not bad at holding my breath to this day, I wonder if this exercise actually helped, well it was fun anyway. I remember one naughty thing I did whilst we lived here, I thought it would be fun to climb out of my bedroom window onto the balcony and light a fire to keep warm, very bad decision indeed, during the day I managed to filch several pieces of coal, some kindling and a fire lighter and a few matches and hide them out on the balcony, behind a big plant pot, I was excited most of the day, of having my own little coal fire on the balcony later that evening, we were still in winter and I can remember quietly putting on my slippers and climbing out of the window and down onto the balcony, I arranged all the items as I had watched my mother do many times, lit a match, the fire lighter caught, and I added more kindling and coal, it started to get nice and warm and the flames got higher it was lovely, all of a sudden there was a scream from behind me, my mum had seen the flickering of the flames through the curtain that covered the balcony door threw it open to reveal me in my pyjamas smiling proudly, of course I had no thought of how I was going to extinguish the flames once my dabbling into pyrotechnics was over. The door open followed by a whoosh as bowl of cold water extinguished the flames and me, I was dragged inside by mum in tears, dad who wanted to skin me alive and me trying to think of a suitable excuse why I had done this, spontaneous combustion?, aliens, a stray meteor, hmm I can think of many reasons now but at the time I kind of stood there soaking wet shivering and close to tears, I was put in a hot bath and clean warm pyjamas and marched back to bed, with the threat of a good spanking if this ever happened again, Dad was a very fair man and only the threat of a spanking was enough for me not to try this again.

On Saturday afternoons we used to go and visit my Nan, my dad's mom, she still lived in the "two up, two down" house in Lozells, this was a bit of a tradition as dad came from a large family and it was the only time I got to see my cousins, considering it was a large family there was a lot of internal feuding between the siblings, you would have thought they would have been more close than they were sadly not, I have cousin's to this day that I can barely remember, one particular sticks in my mind, my cousin had asked mom to go around for coffee one afternoon, they lived in walking distance from where we lived, in fact just passed the shops where I used to go to school, I think I was around seven years old, I can remember arriving at this nice house, and being greeted warmly by my cousin Pat or "Patty" as she was known to me, it was there I met her daughter Karen, I remember her being a very sweet quiet girl, we ran up the stairs to play with her toys, as I entered the room I can remember stopping and thinking "Dolls", she had dolls everywhere, I had boys things you know a train set etc, but she had dolls, we sat down on the floor, and bless her dear heart she rummaged through her doll collection and found me a boy doll to play with, this was just before a very famous boys action figure doll came out, so I guess I was at the cutting edge of doll "evolution" for boys, we sat and played for around an hour or so before mum came to fetch me to go home, I can remember Karen gave me the doll to keep, and vividly remember holding my mom's hand turning back and waving as walked back towards home, that was the first, and last time I ever saw her, I have tried to find her, just to say hello, and see how she is getting along but without success, with most of the family now deceased, and the rest not knowing each other because of the family at loggerheads over something that we the children knew nothing about, it has left us not knowing each other, and isolated, I think she stuck out in my mind so clearly as I just remember her being incredibly kind and happy, I did hear some years later that she had gone into the fashion industry, I'm sure her doll collection had some part to play in that, I hope she is well and happy, by the way I named the doll "Rodney" and kept it for many years.

I have a very vivid memory of being at school and not being able to keep up with the work, I must have been seven or eight years old, the teacher called in my mother, and I can remember saying that I could not understand anything she wrote on the blackboard, it turned out that I could not see very well at all, I was taken to the local optician and was prescribed glasses, we did not have much money so I had to have the national health frames which were awful, they were round and had a "horn rimmed" appearance, having glasses turned out to be a double edged sword, I could now see the blackboard perfectly and my work improved, but as we all know back then anyone that was different was immediately bullied, I can still remember all these years later standing in the corner of the school playground, with all the playground chanting "four eyes, "four eyes", and the teachers doing nothing to stop it.

I withdrew into myself, I began to dislike people, and I found that animals gave you love, expected nothing in return, they did not taunt or bully you, and they were much more fun to be around, how cruel children are to each other.

Around this time my asthma got worse, I'm not surprised really lighting fires on balconies, my parents were advised it would be better to move out of the city outskirts to a more rural location, I suppose pollution in those days was a lot worse and to have smog was nothing out of the ordinary, Dad also needed to work, he was a skilled engineer and had worked for the same firm since he was 14 years old, I can remember us taking a trip to Telford, at the time it was a new and growing town, and all I could think of was "this is going to be a long way to come to school and see my friends, Dad went for an interview with an engineering firm at the time I can remember him not being very happy after, years later he told me that the guy interviewing him was only a "kid" in his words, and I'll be f***d if I'm going to work for some snot nosed kid who is barely out of his nappy, dad was ex-army you see he had fought in north Africa so his language was very colourful at times, and he also did not suffer fools gladly.

We went and viewed the house that was on offer, I can remember mum saying she didn't like it I shook my head and I think that was all Dad needed to put Telford firmly in his rear view mirror, none of us ever went there again, Dad certainly never did and woe betide anyone that mentioned Telford.

The next place on offer was Tamworth, at the time still a small market town with many black and white buildings in and around the town centre a lovely big castle, and a home close to a huge parkland that thankfully to this day has not been built on, moving here would mean that dad could commute the distance to his work and he wouldn't have to change his job, nice clean fresh air and acres of parkland for me to explore, but not light fires in, the house was a small terraced three bedroom house with a huge front garden and moderate sized back garden, we actually saw the house plot before it was built and can remember standing looking at the concrete raft on where the house would be built, anyway the house overlooked the park and 30 paces or so away you could be in a different world, birds fruit trees in an old orchard a stream that was full of frogs newts and sticklebacks to me it was like moving to heaven, here I could actually play outside run around and enjoy myself.

My first encounter looking after a bird was "Fred the crow", Fred came into my life one sunny windy summers day, in the park I played as a child there was a group of some eight or ten pine trees, I heard a commotion coming from this direction as I approached I saw a group of older boys throwing stones and sticks at this black blob on the ground which was making an horrendous squawking, as I got closer the boys attention turned on me "what do want four eyes" one cruelly said, now you have to remember I was 10 and these boys were much older than me, 14 maybe 15, I had one thing they did not!!, well two actually I was as thin as a garden rake and was determined!!, so I waited my chance then rushed up to the biggest boy, kicked him right up the cobblers, scooped up the black blob and ran as fast as I could, away from the scene, followed by the usual cruel taunts and a hail of stones and broken branches, I glanced back and the biggest boy who by this time was on his knees clutching his groin, I carried on running, bursting through the back gate at home, I stood for a moment with my palms on my knees, bent over gasping for breath, I sat myself down on the lawn and placed my black bundle on my lap, all I can remember seeing was this huge black beak and the waaaak waaaak waaaak noise, I smiled to myself and thought now what.

Mom and dad came outside to see what all the commotion was about, and immediately fell in love with him and agreed and so "Fred" came to stay, in those days tea chests were easily sourced, and I made myself what was I suppose could be called a night quarters type box, with a chicken wire covered hinged door with a branch wedged across the middle for a perch, Fred turned out to be a crow, I used to scour the garden for worms and grubs for him, his favourite trick when he finally realized what his wings were for was to fly up and chase a tiny rubber power ball that I used to fling at the floor with all my might and he would fly up and catch it as the ball peaked on its journey upwards, and return it to my feet for me to do it again, at the very least 10 times in a row, looking back he must have been incredibly fit.

For the time we had together we were inseparable and best friends, I had always had a sort of affinity with animals especially birds, to me people were always an annoyance and a constant source of disappointment, if you were not useful to them you were cast aside, like an unwanted toy, later in life I was asked by someone, "and what exactly do you suffer from Chris?", I replied with no hesitation "people", I suffer from "people", which apart from my lovely family and a handful of close friends is still true to this day.

In those days it was common place during the long summer holidays to go and play in the vast park, this place in years to come would be vital in my first steps in falconry, the park was literally a stone's throw from my home and opened up a whole world of nature and exciting things to do, for instance there was a small brook running around the perimeter, where almost daily we would take a net, and a jam jar with string around the top to form a handle, we would fish for sticklebacks, newts and frogs this was all before dreaded pollution, the wildlife here was quite prolific, Dragonflies, and the funny little pond skaters, that used to zoom across the water sometimes quite fast, the flow of water back then was much faster than today, not so long ago I went for a walk past it and was horrified to see how overgrown and with rubbish dumped in there, even a shopping trolley, why do we treat our environment in such a way beggars belief.

Exploring the park almost daily in the six weeks holiday was always full of fun, there were new creatures to be found, den's to be built at the base of the thickest hawthorns, on this particular day we ventured a little further, to a field that is now sadly part of an industrial estate, scattered over the field were a few sheets of rusty old corrugated roofing, we used to quietly take the corner and quickly lift it up and flip it over, and if you were lucky you saw a field vole or a wood mouse scamper away, this one day we quickly whipped up a sheet of this rusty metal and there was a nest of wood mice, about 3 feet of so away was a dead adult mouse, which we thought in our young minds must have been the mother, maybe someone had walked over the sheet or maybe some other cause, anyway I decided to take two of them home with me, as boys do.

In our garage was an old fish tank roughly about 4ftx18"x2ft high, this was half carried dragged up into my room soil compost and leaf litter added in layers, while the mice were safely tucked up in another small tank, I made a framework lid and added a tube light fitting with a red bulb, the idea being that I could turn this on at night and watch them from the comfort of my bed, the mice were added and over the following days made it their home making little tunnels sometimes up against the glass.

Now mice are very good at jumping and squeezing through wire mesh as I was to find out when they failed to be visible in there carefully crafted home after a few days, "the little buggers had got out", I had made the top layer of soil too close to the mesh on the top, and used too big a hole mesh size, so we now had two rogue wood mice running around the house loose, I dare not tell my dad and never did, occasionally I saw signs of them around the house but kept quiet.

"The pine trees where I was to find Fred"

2 DARK DAYS

After Fred went away this left a huge hole in my heart, and in my life.

Much worse news was to follow, my mom "Peggy" was diagnosed with Cancer, I myself was 12, when you hear this you are not fully aware of what this means, or what is going on and how painful things will become, for me it was watching my mom who I loved dearly, over the period of around a year sorry I cannot be more accurate on this as I had blotted much of this from memory and recalling this now to share with you is very difficult so I hope you will stay with me, I watched as my mom became progressively weaker, more tired and unable to do most things, it was horrible to witness, dad and I moved a single bed downstairs with a view onto the back garden which she loved to plant flowers in the summer months, and loved to grow sweet peas by the back door, occasionally now I catch the scent of sweet pea flowers and I am immediately transported back to that time with a mixture of sadness and happiness.

I spent as much time with her as I could, sitting on the bed talking playing games and sometimes we even managed to laugh, I can now over 40 years on still remember her face and for that I feel so grateful as an adult I now feel fortunate that I had those 13 years with my mom, they were precious and I am lucky I have those memories some do not have that luxury, but as a child I was angry and bitter and I blamed god as I prayed to him to let her live, and save her and he didn't and I was hurt, why me why us why her, it seemed so wrong, I would wake up, months even years later and run downstairs to see her in the kitchen, making breakfast and throwing her arms around me, thinking in my young mind that it had all been a horrid dream, it was that vivid to me, back then, standing there in my pyjamas slowly realizing that all this had really happened, I have never told anyone this, as I have always found it difficult to talk about.

I can remember the morning so clearly, a Sunday morning, my dad came into my bedroom, gently shaking me awake, as I rubbed my eyes I can remember his words, "she has gone Chris", his words did not sink in, "Gone where" I thought, in my young half asleep mind, I followed him downstairs, still in my pyjamas, to the kitchen where my Brother his wife and my mom's friend were all gathered, the mood was very sad and hung over them like a heavy cloud of despair, I can remember them going in to the room where she lay on the bed, one by one to pay their respects, I clutched onto my dad, "please, I can't go in", I sobbed to him, no one actually said to me it is ok, you don't have to go in, and for years into adulthood I carried this like a guilty secret, I felt so ashamed that I did not go into see my dear my mom, I felt like I had let her down, and let myself and everyone else down too, I just wanted to remember her in my mind as happy and smiling, as she always was even when she must have been in dreadful pain.

The rest of that day was like a horrible dream that I wanted to wake up from, I just sat on my bed sobbing, thinking why my mom, she was a good kind and loving person and my mom and I wanted, no I needed her there with me.

From that day on I distanced myself even more from people, I would not get close to anyone ever again I thought, because no way did I ever want to feel that sad, and empty again, which at 13 makes all the sense in the world, but as an adult I can see how wrong that was, I suppose I put myself into some kind of protection mode, it did not matter what anyone said to me, I did not feel any better, I just sat in my room for three weeks, and all the school thought about was to send around the "wag man" to see why I wasn't at school, my dad had the foresight to go to my school and speak with the headmaster, and explain things, on my return most of the teachers were very kind one or two were awful, we had a maths teacher, Mr Jones, I had fallen that far behind in the subject, I had no clue what algebra was, and his reaction to my tortured muffled attempts to ask for help was to shout at me, I can remember bursting into tears and running all the way home.

From this point onward I pretty much lost interest in everything, a dark curtain fell over our world, and I believe never really lifted again, if it was not for the fact we had an amazing school garden, where I learned to grow Geraniums, and vegetables, I would not have gone back, or fought not too anyway, we had three huge greenhouses and our Teacher was Mr Turner, whose nickname was "Tommy Turner", he was very strict but thank god he saw when people, like me wanted to learn.

Dad did his very best to fill the hole left by mom's passing, but things would never be the same for either of us again.

One morning there was a knock on my door, it was a school friend he opened up rucksack inside were two young kestrels, in hindsight this was wrong but we were young and ignorant.

He said, "one is for you" "They are Kestrels" he said, well it looked anything like a kestrel to me, I had seen them flying over the park where I played and fished, they were graceful and came to a hover before dropping down on some unsuspecting mouse, "what are we going to do with them" I said, I'm gonna train it, came the reply, to do what?, he sighed and said "have you not seen the film Kes?, erm no, I will bring you the book to read, so we agreed he would take both of them home as he had a pen on a shed until I had gathered the necessary items I would need to look after my new charge, I was very excited, and as his word the next day he knocked on my door after school and said here you go have a read of this, I'm off home now to feed the kestrels he said, so I closed the door and sat down on the sofa to read it, as I opened the book, I saw a huge blue stamp in the front saying "Property of T*****H Library", what he had failed to mention to me was that he had gone down town on the bus, to the library asked for the book, then walked out with it under his coat therefore permanently borrowing it!!, so I began to read and can say without question was hooked, I wanted to learn more and a few days later after going to his house several times, well as many as I could fit in to see the birds off to the library I went to find books on falconry, this time in case you are wondering I borrowed them properly with a card, I read everything I could find, my favourite of which at the time was "As the falcon her bells", a book which was to open a whole new chapter in my life.

I found a maker of falconry equipment, Martin Jones, who I still buy from to this day!!, the item I was most excited about getting was a proper falconers glove which Martin custom made, and you had to send a drawing around your hand for sizing, in most of the books I had read people were wearing ex-military leather gloves, RAF high altitude gloves, and even welding gloves, although an expense I decided to start off the right way and get myself a proper one, so after drawing carefully around my spread out hand and fingers, tongue firmly locked between my teeth the way you do when concentrating closely on something worthwhile, I sent off my hand print, and awaited my glove, l had found a Jess pattern and set about making my first pair of Jesse's, anyway to bypass the mundane ins and outs, my young charge came to stay and grew splendidly, and in no time at all was flying free to the lure, I used to wake early each morning and flew her before work, which was a labor intensive mind numbingly boring job at a local fizzy drinks factory, l was lucky as our house was on the edge of a huge public park, in less than 30 seconds I was in a totally different environment of trees lush open green spaces, and best of all "no people", I remember one particular time, it was winter it must have been during the Christmas holidays, I picked my bird up from her weathering out on the tiny back lawn, there was a good covering of snow in the park, and the silence almost hurt my ears, and better still no people to ask silly questions and deter me from my fun, I cast her off into a huge oak tree then began to swing my lure, down she dropped flying towards me, one pass, if memory serves me she did 4/5 passes then I bunged the lure and handle in the air she caught it and came to land safely some 20 yards from me, I was fiddling in my bag for the pickup piece for a minute or so, when I returned my gaze to my bird on the lure I could barely believe what I was seeing, there, sat on the lure were not one but two female Kestrels, I thought I had double vision or something, it must have been that cold, this wild female had saw the meat on the lure and lost all fear over hunger and decided to tuck in as well, and there they sat side by side, feeding from the ample piece of beef I had tied to the lure!!.

I was that flabbergasted I plonked myself down right there in the snow, sitting mesmerized at what I was witnessing, when the wild hawk had took her fill she flew off and left me with a contented feeling that maybe falconry that day had been responsible for saving a wild bird from starvation I never saw that wild kestrel again even though I flew my own bird there in more or less the same spot everyday, she must have made a kill somewhere else and went on to lead a fruitful life as a parent, rearing several broods in her lifetime perhaps, I hope so anyway.

My little kestrel grew stronger with every day that passed, and I even got her to "hover", I would hide the lure behind my back and she would throw upwards in the air and hover above my head, she was truly behaving as she would in the wild.

I love to see wild kestrels hovering in the fields then all of a sudden drop down and catch a mouse maybe, I don't think I could ever grow tired of watching any wild hawk or falcon even today my heart beats faster as soon as I see one, especially watching the sparrowhawks hunting in and around my back garden the way they twist and fly and jink and flip over fences to surprise maybe feeding starlings on the ground the other side, and what still amazes me to this day is that people can walk by a feeding sparrowhawk and not notice them at all under a hedge, maybe there not "tuned" into their surroundings?, from the window in the little room I sit now writing I have watched a wild sparrowhawk plucking her prey, then stop and freeze as someone walks past to catch the bus, then continue as they are out of range, they have probably past within 20 foot or so, incredible.

I regularly saw my old school friend throughout my life we remained firm friends, he would call in occasionally after I was married and talk about the old days when we used to fly our kestrels or go ferreting, I will never forget one Sunday evening, he came to the door and remarked how my hair which was going Grey, in his words he said I looked like a "mad badger", it made me laugh, he would not come in as he normally did for a cup of tea, he said "I just wanted to come and see you" I did not think anything of this at the time, a couple of weeks later I learned that he had been found dead, I was shocked and upset, I cannot say what happened, but his last words still ring inside my head, it was such an awful waste of a life and his death left an indelible mark on my life to this very day.

3 NEW YORK

As I mentioned earlier I worked at the fizzy pop factory, the money was good but the work was hard and very labor intensive, it was my mum's friend who got me the job there, I had pretty much known her all my life and was friends with her sons, she asked me to call round that weekend, I was always round there anyway so it was nothing out of the usual, anyway I went round they were all sitting around the kitchen table and she said to me how do you fancy three weeks in America, I must have stood there with my mouth wide open, erm, "yes please I would love to thank you", they all laughed and I was thinking wow this is amazing, I had never been out of the country before and destinations like this were usually for the rich and famous, her sister had married an American businessman and they had moved over to New York State a place called East Setauket, which wasn't too far from the city of New York, the trip was to take place the end of august beginning of September and I would need a passport, and a suitcase and new clothes, I had to be prized out of jeans back in those days.

We were to fly with Laker Airways, Freddie Laker who had pioneered lo-cost no frills long haul flights to John F Kennedy airport in New York, and we were to fly from Manchester Airport, my passport and visa was applied for and I was all prepared, money had been exchanged a week or so before and all we had to do was wait for the day, a friend of ours from where we worked drove us to the airport, I couldn't believe the plane we were to board, considering how much we paid for the return flights the aircraft was huge, the cabin was very wide indeed and put modern air travel to shame, we took our seats awaiting take off, a few minutes after it was announced there was a delay taking off as we were carrying too much fuel basically the aircraft was overweight and it seemed the solution was to open a valve release the excess fuel and then wash the excess away don't ask, my friends mum had gone white she didn't like flying at the best of times and this added a new dimension of doubt to her already frayed nerves, once this minor inconvenience was out of the way we took off without delay.

Once in the air we looked around the aircraft further, there was even a small staircase up to another small level behind where the cockpit was, I can remember expressing an interest in the aircraft which I believe was a 747 to one of the cabin crew, a Little further into the flight she returned and said would I like to meet the captain?, I would love to so off we headed to the cockpit where the door was wide open sigh, how things have changed, I shook hands with all the crew in turn and spent a good half hour learning all about transatlantic air travel and how the pilots of Laker airways had a different approach to take off, they did not run the engines at full bore for take-off, I later heard that this particular airline company had the best maintained engines of any airline of the day, very impressive.

The rest of the journey passed slowly till finally we arrived at JFK airport, we collected our luggage, passed through customs without any problems and met my friends, Uncle who was to drive us from the airport out to long island where we were to stay.

My first impressions of America were good, I noticed how calm and laid back everything was how different the cars were and how big long and straight the roads were and craning my neck to see the top of the skyscrapers as we past-by, but soon we left the city behind us and were into countryside not unlike our own, I was amazed how close to New York city you could be but still be surrounded by lovely peaceful and green countryside, we were heading for East Setauket which is right by Port Jefferson, and I think if I had to choose anywhere in the world to live it would be here, or a simple house near the Beach in Greece, possibly the latter as I do love Greece and its people, we pulled up at a timber built house set in a third of an acre, where a lady with an Anglo American accent flew down the steps to hug her sister and nephew, she then turned to me and said, "hi you must be Chris" I nodded and she then flung her arms around me kissing me on both cheeks and said you are very welcome and I felt immediately like one of the family and was treated very much like one, I felt at home.

My friend and I were shown to a downstairs room called the den, this led out onto the garden, in this room was a pull out double bed, never having shared a bed with another lad I was a bit dubious but all was well we were all totally exhausted after our long journey, after putting our cases downstairs there was a lovely hot meal waiting for us upstairs where we met our hosts children two boys and a girl, we were as fascinated with them as they were with us accents, clothing etc, we ate and chatted away through our meal, but we were all flagging terribly and soon headed off for bed where we slept right through till 10:00am the next morning.

I awoke the next morning to find the family had eaten breakfast and headed off to school and dad had gone to work in the city he used to leave at 6:00am in the morning to travel by car then train to the city, "would you like some breakfast" my kind host asked, there were cereals pancakes, I think I ate both as I was famished, after breakfast we explored our new surroundings, there was a small above ground swimming pool in a huge back garden, the first few days were rested as we were going to be taken into the city on the weekend it was something to look forward too, after school when the children came home we got to know them a bit better, and a stream of their friends came to the door I suppose they wanted to meet the people from England, they were fascinated how we spoke and the feeling was mutual.

The weekend arrived and the family had planned to take us to Sagamore Hill the home of Theodore Roosevelt, the 26th president of the United States, it wasn't a long drive, but well worth the visit the house and grounds were amazing, we spent a few hours looking around the house and grounds, I had bought some monkey nuts in the shell and was munching away happily enjoying the wildlife, the lovely scenery and the beautiful warm sunshine, a young Grey squirrel sat watching me and when I offered it a nut I fair nearly choked on what erupted next this middle aged American lady launched a tirade of words at me, "don't feed that she said, if it bites you, you will die", don't do it don't, it may have rabies, you will die, hmm a little over reaction on her part I stood back up from my kneeling position, turned to her, with all the composure only an Englishman can summon in such a confusion and said, "I was simply going to toss it a shelled nut", I had no intention of offering it my juggler vein, but I do appreciate your concern, for god's sake I thought, that was a bit over the top, I carried on munching my nuts, and enjoying the park that surrounded this beautiful house.

The following week we took a walk down to the nearest small town which sat on the coast Port Jefferson, it was bloody miles and the weather was warm too, the town reminded me of that little seaside town from a well-known TV murder show, with little white painted wooden stores and shops as we walked past a store there were two guys standing outside a barbers shop they offered us a cigar each.

 Apparently the two of them had just opened the barbers store that day, we tried to explain that we were only visiting the area, but they insisted on us keeping the cigars they proudly showed us around inside, we had both had our haircut a few days before traveling so we couldn't even have a trim, we bid them farewell smoking our cigars, and decided we needed a cold drink so we popped into a shop and bought 4 cans of Budweiser beer each, we set off back home, happily drinking the beer, when from behind us we heard a woop, woop, it was only a police car, he pulled alongside us, we looked at each other as if to say huh?, what have we done, the officer from inside said, "do you know it is illegal to drink in the street?", I said I didn't, he said you are not from around here are you? No we replied, apparently you can drink from a brown paper bag in the street, but of course in America we were underage too although both over 18 you have to be 21 to drink alcohol we were apologetic and felt a little sad as he confiscated the beer from us, I bet he drank them when he got home too, what annoyed me more than anything you could walk round smoking a cigar in public so why not drink a cold beer?, oh well all ended happily eventually we got home by which time we were absolutely shattered, the family were gob smacked when we told them where we had walked to, as everyone just drove everywhere, we thought it best not to mention the beer episode, we had learned our lesson.

The next weekend we were taken into New York city, we followed the route that Betty's hubby took to work, parked the car at the local train station and rode that into the city, I don't think I have ever seen such a busy place, New Yorkers are very forthright people and say exactly what they mean and are impatient to a fault, a saying that always amuses me depicts this rather aptly, "can you tell me the way to the statue of liberty, or should I f**k myself right here?", hilarious, and the taxi drivers too so rude we just laughed at them, and it went completely over our heads, we saw a group of police officers standing around a squad car, and we asked politely if we could have our pictures took with them, they were a hoot and really made us feel welcome, one of them I got talking too, who was referred to by the others as "Duke" told me that in his entire career as a New York police officer, he never once had to draw his gun in anger, which surprised us all as we tend to think this would be an almost daily occurrence.

The next stop was to be the Empire State Building, which I really wanted to go up, but with a fear of heights I knew was going to be a struggle, we boarded a high speed elevator and I immediately put my feet round the edges, just like James bond did in one of his films, my logic told me that if the floor disintegrated below me at least I could hang onto the rail, with my feet clinging on for dear life round the edge, what a plonker.

Once we got to the top the view was breathtaking from the observation deck, there was a wall some 5ft high that until the previous year had no bars running along the top, apparently too many people were jumping off, it took me ten minutes before I could even contemplate going anywhere near the wall to look out, it made me feel that giddy, I managed to take a few photos before standing well back, we spent about 45 minutes up there before heading off towards the Statue Of Liberty a must see for any tourist to New York, we travelled by taxi to catch the boat over to Liberty Island, the crossing was a short bumpy wet one I was glad to set foot on Terra firma, I have always got terribly sea sick and I was just about to throw up as we docked.

We made our way over to the statue which seemed smaller to me than you imagine in pictures, a lady told us they had closed off the torch that day so we couldn't go right to the top as it was too windy, the queue was horrendous and we waited in line, we actually managed to get halfway up before our host and Guide Pat said time was getting on and we really needed to get moving back homeward, but at least we had seen the statue and climbed halfway up the inside.

Before we knew it our Holiday was over and it was time to fly back to reality and the daily dirge of the fizzy pop factory, which I was not looking forward to at all, I had made up my mind to move on.

4 FINDING THE FALCONRY CENTRE

After flying my little kestrel for just over a year I realized that it would be nice to catch something, and that to do this Was important to approach it properly, remembering the book I had read sometime before quickly remembered there was reference to a tiny market town called Newent, and a falconry centre buried in the beautiful Gloucestershire countryside and so began to plan a trip to this location, in those days there was no Internet let alone google earth and I wasn't even sure if the place still existed just a wisp of a myth from an old book, but I was determined to find out. From where I lived a one mile walk to the train station, alight, or get off at Gloucester, wait and catch a bus from Gloucester to Newent, alight again in Newent town centre, and from their asking directions, right that was it all on paper now to put into operation. It was a nice warm summers day I chose a Saturday, and off I went with spam sandwiches, a can of fizzy pop my penknife and an apple, oh and course enough money to get me there and back plus a little extra to spend while there, if indeed the place itself was still in existence!, the book had been written 10 years before, So with hope in my heart and my British weather survival kit I set off positive in mind and hopefully luck on my side.

My journey started with a 1 mile walk to the local train station, where I boarded a train to Birmingham, there I was to change to a train that would take me as far as Gloucester, have you ever noticed people that regularly travel on trains, I think it is there mission not to speak to anyone during their journey and carry themselves around the carriage with an air of superiority as they visit the loo and the buffet car for some British Rail tea, I think mainly because I have always been a people watcher I like to put a story behind a person's journey, Miss X who sat opposite me constantly fixing her hair and makeup was she traveling to meet a lover, or even maybe an audition for a part in a west end show?, Mr X who sat adjacent to me reading the Times with his mac and umbrella was he in fact a secret agent traveling by rail to London and hopefully by using the trains lessen the risk of him being followed to his final rendezvous, all this helped the journey along and gave me much amusement, I disembarked the train at Gloucester station, I knew from here it was going to have to be a bus, luckily the bus station was not far and I made inquiries and was told where to catch the bus to Newent, it was due in within the next 20 minutes which was very welcome, the bus arrived I boarded and sat again watching the people, finally arrived at Newent, a lovely little market town, as I left the bus I asked passer-by, "excuse me do you know of a falconry centre nearby", and waited with bated breath, "yes dear", came the reply " follow this road and it is on the left", "about a mile", by this time it was almost lunchtime, and I wasn't there yet!!.

I followed Watery Lane, and out of the distance I saw a familiar image from the book, this time as a signpost on the side of the lane, my heart raced, made it. Entering the car park, next to the house was a wooden fronted building, I saw up high in the wall above, and behind a barred window, I could see a falcon sitting basking in the warm sunshine. Walking through the door into what was a small museum and shop sat behind a long was a girl her friendly voice greeted me "Hello just the one", Later I found out this was Dinah one of Phillip Glasier's daughters, a conversation followed about my epic journey to reach the centre, anyway through the double doors past the long counter was the "Hawk Walk", there was every kind of bird you could imagine I had only ever seen drawings of!!, my favourites I think was Sable the Golden eagle, Mozart the eagle owl, lanner falcons, and a little sparrowhawk sitting on a bow perch, which was of particular interest because this is what I was looking at flying next, because it was possible to hunt with one, and where my home was a flight would be easily found, especially in my little park retreat.

Then a female voice broke the idyllic quiet, calling "Wanker, Wanker, where are you", I immediately felt at home, and in like-minded company, I later found out that "Wanker" in fact was a cat and the disembodied, voice was Mima herself. A bird was being flown so hurriedly I made my way to the flying ground where I saw a lanner falcon flown, I can only describe the feeling as "uplifting" as the falcon stooped time and time again, sometimes flying out of sight then "HO" shattered the air, then high up out of the distance appeared the falcon first as a tiny black dot then closer wings folding and the air literally screaming as it rushed at speed through her primary wing feathers, at the very last moment the lure (a pair of old wings garnished with a piece of beef) was hurled high into the air where the falcon feet first hit the lure with a resounding "smack", bringing her safely to a controlled and gently to the ground, the beauty elegance and gracefulness at what I had just witnessed, was so emotional it brought a tear to my eye.

In all I think I was able to stay that day for around 3 hours before beginning the mammoth trek home.

I arrived home that evening fired up to make my little kestrel fly like the lanner falcon I had seen flown twice that day, this was the first of many more, day and weekend visits.

One my second visit I took two friends with me both of which had an interest in birds of prey, we arrived early about an hour well before opening, I was that keen to see more, my companions were grumbling as to why we had gotten up so early, I ignored them and tucked into a cheese sandwich.

Opening time!, the door was unlocked and we entered, Dinah said "back again "smiling we paid and made our way through to the hawk walk seeing even more birds I had never seen before after about half an hour or so we came back up through the hawk walk and who was standing there? Only the man I had read so much about who had moved his whole family to Gloucestershire to open the Falconry Centre, Philip Glasier and there he stood right in front of me, I already had a huge amount of respect for this man so as one does stood there like a lemon and speechless.

He was talking to a party of people who were also visiting that day, so we thought we would tag along on the tour, as we trotted along, me hanging on every word spoken hoping to glean the slightest morsel of falconry advice my friend turned to me and said, where have you left your kestrel today? I replied, "inside on her screen perch" well, although this comment was just over a whisper, the great man himself heard it, he stopped talking peered straight at me and said, "anyone still using a screen perch needs there head looking at", everyone was staring at me, I had gone bright red, and was frozen to the spot, "shit" I thought, of all the possible ways I could have met my "falconry hero" this had to be the worst, tail between my legs we carried on our visit, waving goodbye to Dinah we headed back home.

Several more visits came and went, on one particular occasion I was ushered through the back to use the house toilet I passed woman in a purple quilted coat feeding a chocolate digestive biscuit to sheep saying something like, "oh come on Ow take it if you want it", as I passed I said, a cheerful "Hello!!" As if this was the most normal thing to witness on your way to the loo, the woman was in fact, "Bill" Phillips wife.

I gradually got to know the family better and the months passed and the year grew old, looking back I think seeing the Glasier's and being with them was the family life I so dearly missed, I had become very introverted and shy since the death of my mother, but slowly I was coming through this, I still couldn't be bothered with most people, and there expectations of me, but here I felt I could be myself.

On my next visit Dinah said to me, "we are running a course early next year, why don't you come?", so I took the paper folded it neatly put it in my bag carefully then promptly lost it on my way home.

"oh bullocks" I grumbled.

On the next visit a fresh form was obtained, and I sat and read it the fee then was £160 and the course was over a two week period 10 days in all with the weekend in between free, great!! I thought I can help out on the free days over the weekend, now £160 doesn't sound much these days but back then I was only earning £32 slaving away in the grotty pop factory I hated it there, anyway I worked out my finances like any 19 year old would, and after paying my board to my dad I could just about do it, oh and I also had to find money, For lodgings as the course was non-residential, so I paid my deposit, and Dinah recommended some lodgings, and all was in place for the following January.

Christmas and new year came and went with the usual lacklustre, dad did his best but Christmas would never be the same again.

I packed up what I needed in a black holdall, brief pause while we change coaches this one is even more bumpy thank god for auto spelling check doo daa.

So all packed up I headed for the train station, it was nearly the end of January and the weather was cold frosty dark nights in fact everything to keep people indoors and away from me.

I arrived at my lodgings in Newent, a huge spacious farmhouse, I was met by a lovely quiet family, shown to my room then invited down for a hot Sunday meal with them, now to many this may seem a very insignificant and everyday event, but to me this indeed was a very special and treasured event, it had now been more than 6 years that I had sat down to a proper family meal and I confess I felt a little wooden and self-conscious, I did my best to hide this from my kind hosts.

The evening passed quietly in front of a huge roaring fire then up to bed for an early start, I can remember turning out the light before sleep for the very first time, it was pitch black, I had grown up in towns and cities and had never experienced this kind of darkness before, I can remember thinking what if I need a wee in the night?, well I was young and in possession of a good bladder so thankfully this problem never arose.

I awoke the next morning bright and early and without the aid of a "safety net", ablutions taken care of I toddled down the huge staircase and made my way to the kitchen, the family were all there tucking into various cereals and toast, and I followed suit, breakfast as I remember was a quiet affair, which was fine with me.

The lady of the house had kindly made me up an ample packed lunch, which I stuffed into my coat pocket, and off I went.

The lanes were quite frosty that morning, and I marvelled at the wonderful patterns the frozen spider webs made in the hedgerows as I passed by them, hoping I didn't see the webs creators, I have a terrible fear of spiders, which was compounded by a very insensitive friend who thought it would be hilarious to place his pet tarantula on my left shoulder a few years earlier, whilst visiting him at his home, pause while I just check underneath my desk for spiders as already my skin has begun to crawl.

I arrived at the museum door as a few other members of the course were arriving the first person I met was Andrew, he was some sort of horse dealer working in and out of the middle east, he got the nickname "Handy Andy" he drove a little MG sports car or a "tart trap" as it soon became known, he was a very well-spoken and kind man, the next two people I met were Phillip and Simon they both along with me eventually worked at the Centre and we became from that day firm friends.

Phillip appeared through the double doors, smoking a cigar and took us down to the house into the "Hawk Room" and we all sat around a table with writing pads and me pencil poised to record every syllable possible that came from our mentors mouth.

We went in turn around the table in turn stating our names and when it came to me I swear I heard him mutter under his breath, "hmmm screen perch" lighting his cigar we continued with our first steps into falconry, even then I realized what a privilege it was to be taught by this man.

During our course we each were assigned our own young Kestrel to train, fly and look after, mine was a little "pip" and responded well to every step of her training and I had her loose by the end of the first week, I was very pleased.

One particular day I was to be be in trouble again with the big boss, a few days earlier we had been taught the correct way to make and use a lure which is basically a handle, braided cotton line a pair of old wings with a nice juicy piece of meat on the end, now the ones we were taught with had little sand bags on the end to give weight, replacing the wings and the meat, me oh no, from the weighing room that used to be at the top end of the hawk walk I started to set up my lure and in my eagerness and not thinking at all, began to walk down the hawk walk to the flying ground swinging the lure and whistling without a care in the world, happy to be alive, what I began to realize that all the display falcons in there compartments down each side of the hawk walk were bating furiously towards me, and so did someone else, someone else in fact high up, someone else who had already pulled me up for using a screen perch, I don't think I should write here the tirade of words that rained down on me like a shower of arrows or no one would publish this book fingers crossed it does though, what I can tell you is my head almost disappeared into my shoulders with embarrassment, I quickly put the lure away in my hawking bag and scuttled off as fast as I could into the flying ground to get some lure swinging practice in.

Every morning when we arrived we would go to the little building behind the weighing room where all the little night quarter boxes were, we would pick up our kestrels and put them out to "weather", which simply means putting them out on their little block perches to enjoy some fresh air, and a bath offered in the mornings, the bath consisted of a round large shallow dish, rather like a huge plastic saucer, but in winter taken away before lunchtime so they didn't decide to get wet just before we continued their training, therefore spoiling the training session, and of course being put back well before dusk, Wet" in the night quarter boxes, not a good thing in the cold winter months, in the door was a peephole, which you could look through to make sure no one was ahead of you either putting their bird to bed or retrieving them in the mornings to be blocked out.

I remember one morning as I approached the door hearing the oddest of one sided conversations, "your naughty aren't you?", came the words, I looked through the peephole and to my horror and total astonishment, one of the other persons on the course who shall remain nameless, was tapping his bird around the head repeating, "your naughty aren't you?", this sickened me to the core, I ran and told Dinah what I had witnessed, she immediately, came with me, and saw this for herself, we were both gob smacked, at that moment he appeared out of the door, I am sure we both gave him the filthiest of looks, and by his demeanour realized that we had been watching him, Dinah found her father and the person in question was called in for a one to one chat with Phillip, he was never seen again thank god, I am telling this story not to shame belittle or smear anyone, but to make the point that falconry, and birds of prey are not for everyone, and this kind of behaviour is rare, as this is the only time in my life I have witnessed any kind of ill treatment and abuse towards a bird.

As the course went along young Phillip, Simon and myself were doing more together, later on when we three would return to the Centre at weekends, or the occasional week stay there to help out we acquired the nickname, "The Three Musketeers", I suppose because we were always there at hand, bright eyed and bushy tailed eager and ready to help in an instant!, we would help each other with the things maybe one of us wasn't sure about, let me tell you 5 people in a field all trying to learn to swing a lure has its moments, whack a sandbag behind the head followed by a "sorry" and a roar of laughter from the group, the course was very professional may I add, but had a loose and relaxed feel, perfect environment, and as we found out as our course progressed Phillip was not only a very accomplished falconer, but a very good teacher as well, it can be very had to pass on knowledge if you don't have a "feel" for teaching.

I remember a guy there called Paul, he flew a Merlin to the lure, merlin's are so small and fast and have a tiny turning circle to swing a lure accurately fast and precise as he did was almost art in motion, I used to stand there with my mouth open watching, I felt very privileged to see some of the things that were going on there, and still do to this day, hmm how did I get onto merlin's, oh well let me try and get back on track.

By the end of the course the "Three Musketeers" all had our kestrels loose and flying free, it is a very rewarding feeling and also a nerve wracking one the first time your bird goes free, and that feeling for me stays the same every time, as we became more proficient we were allowed to put a few of the birds away to bed at night, I can remember us all wanting to take turns to put the tiny American kestrel to bed, a sweet little bird and so cute and tiny and we felt trusted and part of the daily goings on.

The course drew to a close, we said our goodbyes, gathered our notes and training charts, (which I still have somewhere), I came away a more confident person and a much wiser one, then it was back to reality and the grotty old pop factory again boohoo.

Later that month the three of us were told we could pick up the kestrels we had trained and they were ours to keep, I was over the moon and made arrangements to go and pick her up.

Because of the winter months and the very short days my journey was a matter of traveling all the way to the Centre, with my cardboard box picking my bird up and immediately turning round and heading back, I met young Phillip there who was on the course with me, and had made arrangements to stop overnight at his parents home just outside Hereford, I stayed the night and after breakfast the next day his parents very kindly took me into Hereford town to catch the bus, I thanked them for the lift, and set about finding the right bus stop I found where too wait, and waited patiently for the bus to pull in, I think it was only something like a 15 minute wait before the bus pulled in and was able to board.

We had only been traveling a short while when it began to snow, how lovely and Christmas I thought, and it kept snowing, getting thicker and thicker as we travelled onward, we arrived in Kidderminster where the bus driver promptly announces, in a broad Gloucestershire accent, "sorry Folks I caaan't go any further", "oh great" I thought, here I am miles from home, I had no money apart from small change, I had a kestrel in a cardboard box, what the hell was I going to do, the bus driver didn't give a hoot that I had to get back to Tamworth.

By this time it was getting dark, It is surprising when you are in tight spot how resourceful you can be, I thought right first thing contact home and let dad know what was going on, and he wasn't home, so I managed to get through to someone in the end and they said stay put, the only solution was for them to send out a taxi from Tamworth to pick me up, and don't forget there was heavy snow "everywhere", a taxi driver was found that was willing to come and fetch me, but this was going to take time in the weather, this was all done from a phone box in the middle of Kidderminster, "where will you be" a voice said I had to think quick "the laundrette" I replied giving directions from the phone box, I thought it is warm and dry and that's all I need.

I knew that the laundrettes in those days had a sort of one way lock you couldn't get in but you could get out, so I used this to my advantage, I went and sat inside.

Various people came and went with the odd "shame, hope you get home safely", well I was buggered if I couldn't, If that taxi driver had forgotten about me would I still be sitting on top of that drier, mummified with a cardboard box on my lap, shudders at the thought, the last person left and around 6:30 ish the lights in the shop went off, on a timer I'm guessing, well at least I was relatively warm and dry, I sat tight in the dark, I think the taxi arrived around 7:30-8:00pm ish as his head light beams penetrated the darkness inside the shop I gave a sigh of relief, he waved and I walked out into the cold air then the welcoming warmth of the car, "thank you, Thank you so much" I said, he just smiled and handed me a bottled drink and a sausage roll, that man had even thought to bring me a drink and something to eat, how kind I thought.

The journey back was slow and tedious, I think it was at that point I started to appreciate human company, and that all people did not have an "agenda", I arrived home fed my new little charge and headed for bed, for those of you wondering, the taxi fare was £35, I was earning £32 a week, the driver kindly agreed to let me pay him back in two instalments, thankfully, over the next couple of weeks.

5 THE THREE MUSKETEERS

As the year grew warmer Phillip, Simon and myself visited the Centre as often as possible, meeting up at weekends, Philip lived not too far away near Hereford, Simon in Essex, me in Staffordshire, as I still do to this day, we would help out doing any odd jobs that needed doing, Raking up leaves, taking visitors down to the loo, and were always first in the flying ground for the demonstrations, the three of us remained firm friends for many years, each of us working there as part of the staff at different times never at the same time sadly it was around this time I met Ray and his wife Winnie, they hailed from Totowa, New Jersey, Ray was closer to my age so in that respect we had a lot in common, except a wife of course I was far too young, and the word married scared me to death as it would most men of 19, (checks behind me for irate wife), we would cut the grass and help to build any new pens which was always fun when there are a few of you, then as soon as it was flying time we would drop what we were doing and run down to the flying ground sit and watch the flying displays.

Occasionally the background silence was broken from behind the scenes and mostly out of range of the public, the dis embodied voice called, "Wanker, "Wanker", Mima had lost her cat again!, this always sent the three of us into fits of giggles.

As I am writing this it has just been announced on the TV news that Robin Williams the actor and comedian has died, he had battled with severe depression for many years, I feel for him and is family as this is an awful illness, and can strike anyone at any age regardless of wealth, race or social standing, my thoughts go with him and his family at this sad time.

Where were we?, ah yes the Three Musketeers, "Aladdin's cave", this is where all the tools were kept lawn mowers and every kind of tool you could imagine, "if it wasn't in there you didn't need it", there was also this really useful 4 wheeled cart that we used to transport the various tools around on, so if you were working on a pen across the other side of the centre you could load up the cart and take it all in one go and saved you walking 100 yards or so back for a screwdriver or hammer!, which never worked out that way as there was always some tool you needed to walk back for. The three of us made plans to spend a week down at the centre, Simon's parents had a very nice touring caravan, and they very kindly agreed to bring it down and park it right at the back of the car park for us to stay in, we agreed a week and holiday was duly booked at the pop factory of doom, I couldn't wait to get away from the noisy machinery and the mind numbing boredom for a whole week!!.

The week soon came around, the weather was warm and sunny and we all met up, spending our days helping around and clambering to see who would put the little American kestrel to bed that night, and our evenings spent talking, listening to music and on the odd occasion walking down into Newent to buy a Chinese from the takeaway there, it was a good walk, I'm guessing at least a good country mile, possibly even more which is nothing at all at that age, I wish I could have my 19 year old knees back!, we would bring back the takeaway to the caravan to eat, I wonder if that chinese takeaway restaurant is even still there?, it would be nice to think so.

6 A TIME OF CHANGE

At home my personal life had become quite difficult, my dad had started seeing a woman from where he worked, I can see now why he felt the need to move on, but at the time was shocked and upset and saw this as if this woman was going to replace my mom, I only wish I had the experience and wisdom I have now back then, I'm sure things would not have gone as far as they did.

I was determined that I was not going to like this woman and I did my damnedest not to, what made things worse was that she had 4 children in tow, good god I thought more bloody people I need to interact with, there had only ever been me and my brother, and worse still they were horrendous children, bad mannered, uncouth and absolutely had nothing to contribute to the human gene pool, I remember being forced and virtually dragged to go on a so called "family outing", the outing was doomed from the start, As I remember it was a day trip in the car to a seaside town, it is actually quite difficult for me to recall as I blocked this era in my life out, from the moment the car door was opened they were off, best way I can describe them is "Feral" if children can actually be feral god only knows, I just stood there watching them as they wreaked havoc, took little notice of their mother trying to contain them and even less notice of my poor dad who was stuck between a rock and a hard place, I felt sorry for him, this man had gone through WW2 as a royal signals dispatch rider, he had survived being bombed in the factory where he worked as an engineer just before being called up for service, in fact in that very bombing raid his friend had run in one direction, he had run the other, his friend was killed and dad had survived, the only outer scar was that his hair had turned white within a few weeks, he had even survived Hitler and terrorists in Palestine, but these scruffy little urchins no, I just had the picture in my mind of how many of them it would be possible to pick off with controlled bursts of machine gun fire, or if a bull whip and chair in cartoon like lion tamer fashion would bring them under control, I came to the decision it would not.

On the way back in the car one of them turned to my dad and said, "does pork come from a cow", I just put my face in the palms of my hands and thought good god, it was enough to make you weep, I thought is this going to be my life from now on?.

Thankfully they planned many more holidays and day's out, all of which I managed to wriggle out of mainly I'm sure my dad was convinced that things would have got out of hand and an argument or worse break out, this in hindsight was a bad thing, as I withdrew deeper into myself, became less sociable, possibly the only times I left the house was to go to work, fly my little kestrel, and make my treasured precious visits to the Centre, where all my troubles and worries were out of sight, and I could be myself, and I wasn't that weird kid who flies birds.

With my newly learned knowledge I had gained from my course I felt confident enough to take on a sparrowhawk, I knew this was the right hawk to choose as I would be able to find a flight for her pretty much 20 paces from my front door in the park, we were in July at this point and I knew that within a few weeks the young hawks would be tootling out on the branches and exploring their surroundings.

Near to where I live is some beautiful mixed woodland,(I made many trips to this woodland even camping there to watch wild sparrowhawks, which I will go into later) at the highest point there is still to this day a large section of Scots pines, I thought this would be a good place to look, so off I set with some sandwiches, binoculars, and begin the two mile walk to the woodland.

I arrived at the start of the wood and thought this would be a good time to stop for a break, so I settled myself under a shady tree to eat my picnic as I sat there amongst the wild flowers on the edge of a rolling meadow, which lifted in a gentle slope in front of me I heard the familiar call of a sparrowhawk, it is hard to put it into words but imagine squeezing a squeaky toy really fast, once heard though never forgotten I knew then I might well be in luck, refreshed from my break I pushed on quietly and methodically up the hill towards the area of pine trees, as I entered the the area of Scots pines I was aware of a female spar calling not too far off, so I sat down quietly with my binoculars.

I watched as the female flew into the wood and landed in a pine tree with a funny sort of flat top with an elbow shaped branch just below the canopy of foliage, "what a perfect place for a sparrowhawk to nest" I thought, it was obvious she was feeding a number of chicks it was hard to discern how many even through binoculars, but I counted three heads bobbing about, and they looked pretty well developed, I thought to myself it won't be long before these are climbing about on the branches and then flying, it was at this point I made a very difficult and crucial decision, it was so very tempting to come back and take a wild female, train her hunt with her then release her back to the wild to breed and raise her own family, at the time period I am talking about it was not legal to take a bird from the wild, DDT had done that much damage to the wild sparrowhawk population in the 1960's, wild sparrowhawks were still very much in recovery, although saying this you could argue that if you took a wild bird from the nest, it would be less of a load on the parent birds, and would give the remaining offspring a better chance of survival, anyway this was all hypothetical as I had decided to go and purchase a close rung captive bred bird instead.

In the late 1970's there used to be a bird paper you could buy weekly, or might have been fortnightly I cannot remember and search through the classified ads of birds for sale, a breeder was found, telephoned and collection arranged for a few weeks ahead of time, I had the forethought to make and take with me a set of Jesse's, (the leather straps that are fitted around each leg as a means of holding, and safely controlling a bird, especially when still pretty wild, rather like a dogs collar and leash on a dog for non-falconry people).

I arrived home with her safely in a cardboard box I reached inside and up she popped onto my fist, she tried to fly off a couple of times when I coughed, as you always seem to do at the most inappropriate time, what I noticed about her right away was her eyes so big and round, she was a pip, I will skip the details of training as this has been covered by many people many times and with far more accuracy and detail than I could ever explain, so I will leave it those who teach, and teach well.

I never gave her a name as nothing ever seemed appropriate for her, as her manners improved, so did her progress, daily training used to take place in the local park usually for me by necessity early morning to avoid people and some of the silly questions you get asked, you would be surprised at what your asked, back in those days before council cuts and whatever have you the park was patrolled by a "park keeper", the man in question had chased me off on more than one occasion as a child for throwing sticks up the trees to get conkers, I believe this practice has stopped now due to health and safety, I think that if conkers were played in schools today the pupils would need to don hard hats goggles ear protection, a dust mask leather apron and gloves, maybe even steel toe capped boots, and there would probably be someone that would compile a "risk assessment" on "the playing of conkers in the playground" by "JR Hartley" indeed, lost my thread now, oh yes, the "Park Keeper".

I had reached the stage where I was calling off my sparrowhawk to the fist, this is where you hold a piece of meat on a gloved hand and hope that the bird flies to you and not in the opposite direction, in the middle of the park is a huge white house with an old iron fence around it, some three feet high, yes I still use feet and inches bugger metric and progress, which was the perfect height to perch my little sparrowhawk on and wind out the creance to the desired distance, depending on how far one was along with training, a creance is basically a long safety line wound in a figure of eight on a stick when not in use, so there I am in the park, sparrowhawk on fence, winding out the line when who ambles across to talk to me? You got it the bloody park keeper, "oh wonderful" I thought here we go, oncoming lecture alert, caught red handed, he came across to me and to my total astonishment asked me, "have you seen a young chap flying a bird of prey in this park", without thinking and being totally honest I said "no I haven't" which was totally true I had not seen anyone flying a bird of prey in the park, never ever, yes I had seen dog owners letting their dogs crap everywhere and not pick it up, but never that!, just picture the scene for a moment, me, standing there with 20 yards, (see no metric here), of line at my feet, a leather glove on my left hand one of Martin Jones fine small hawking bags on my right hip and a sparrowhawk perched on the fence to my left side with a close cropped hedge behind her sitting there possibly thinking, "well stop talking and let's get on with it", the fact of the matter was that he had failed to spot my bird and anything odd about my appearance which goes to prove another point, if you are not aware of birds of prey you can completely miss nature at its best, the awkward conversation continued, "because" he quoted, "it is against the byelaw's", oh I said, "he is around here somewhere" he said, anyway "goodbye" he says, "goodbye" I says, I still wonder to this day had I been swinging a lure with my kestrel in chase would the outcome have been any different?, I will leave it for you to decide, we finished our training session then it was home for a cup of tea and a good chuckle at what had just happened.

Training was continued and completed, and I finally had the little spar coming loose from a good distance and pretty much instantly, the year was growing it was early September, and time to go out hunting, as I lived on the edge of the park it was the ideal location to start her off, being ever vigilant looking for the park keeper, he would have made a great SAS trooper as he seemed to have the uncanny ability to be standing right behind you even in the middle of a wide open space, even when you were keeping an eye open for him!, if anyone knows how this is achieved please let me know, as it is a skill I would love to learn.

I had already discovered that if you have a sparrowhawk on your gloved hand, or fist, if they spot something that they fancy for dinner there is a good chance they will try to chase them and end up hanging upside down resembling a fruit bat rather than one of natures skilled little hunters, this is because they dig there claws in and of course results in the "fruit Bat" effect, this is not a technical term by the way but my own description, so there is a technique where you can throw or launch the little bird from the hand also giving her a good head start, the way of throwing a spar has been covered in falconry books, once you get the hang of it is a much better way, you basically end up holding your sparrowhawk or spar as the female is known across your right hand palm imagine touching your right shoulder with the back of your right hand and the bird laying across your palm facing forward and you gently curling your fingers over her sides and over the edges of her back, I hope that gives you a mental picture of how it is done, I know, imagine holding a spear, if you look in Jack Mavrogordato's book, A Hawk for the Bush", you will find a superb drawing in there.

In my experience it takes a little time for the bird to get used to this but once they know the score that they are being gently launched towards there dinner they soon settle into the idea.

I had so much fun that winter, sneaking along hedgerows watching in awe as she would chase and sometimes catch something, I am not sure if I am unique in this as I do not mix with other falconers generally, but I get as much pleasure out of seeing my bird chase and miss it's quarry, as I do if she catches something, if I am honest I'm rooting for the prey to escape, I also think what I enjoy most about flying and hunting with a hawk is that really we are spectators in a totally natural process, as I have said previously this isn't a falconry book, and everything in here is my own experience.

I cannot put into words how much fun I had with that little hawk over that winter, it was only through Phillip Glasier's teaching that had given me the confidence to arrive at the point I did, finally I was practicing proper falconry hunting and catching "sometimes" prey in their natural environment, and for that I would be eternally grateful.

"The park nearby where I used to train my little Sparrowhawk"

7 MOVING ON

By now it was around April and I was hunting with my little spar as often as work allowed, and I am going to admit now, I took as many days off as possible from the horrible pop factory to fly my little hawk, as many times as I could without getting into trouble, as I still needed to clothe myself and pay dad my board money each week, dad as I said earlier was ex-army and from a child it was drummed into me to pay your way in life and also work hard, oh and get up early in the mornings and start your day with a good breakfast, and woe betide you if you wasn't up, washed and dressed by 8:00am or you would get a cold flannel round the back of the neck while you slept, if anyone has suffered this you will know how quickly you shoot out of bed to your feet, try it on a loved one, if you dare, it certainly is a startling way to wake.

Sadly the relationship between my dad and myself had broken down to the point where we hardly spoke, he was spending weekends, and most nights of the week with the "new family", and I felt left out and pushed out, it is one thing to lose your mother as a child but even worse I think to lose your father to a new fresh family, it kind of makes you feel second hand and second best.

I had been at the pop factory in all for around 2 and a half years, and I couldn't take the monotony of it any longer, yes there were opportunities to move up within the company, but pop wasn't for me.

I'm not quite sure what snapped inside me and drove me to make the decision that I did, but this is how it happened, I woke early one Monday morning, packed my black holdall with the few clothes I owned, ate breakfast, sat at the kitchen table, wrote out my notice for work, addressed it, stuck a stamp on it, and without looking back locked the back door and off I headed towards the train station, maybe it was some kind of breakdown, I wasn't emotional the feeling was there was nothing here for me anymore, I felt un-loved and unwanted my "proper" breakdown came many years later, but something drove me out the house that day, anyhow, dad was working nights, and I'm ashamed to say this but I didn't even leave a note I was that angry with him, I passed a post box on my way to the train station, posted my notice, there was no going back now, I followed my usual route to the Centre which was by now second nature to me, and I arrived at the "Falconry Centre", bag in hand.

By this time I had come to know all the family well, Dinah was surprised to see me on a week day, as best as I can remember I chatted in the museum with her, then Phillip appeared a conversation followed, and I was now working there, I am convinced that if I had not been given an opportunity that day I would have ended up god knows where, or even worse, I'm sure Mima had a hand in me being allowed to stay on and work there, so I would like to thank her from the bottom of my heart for that chance.

My first task that day was to clear out the weeds and undergrowth behind the "Hawk Walk" compartments, the side nearest the house, so that we could build extra pens on the space there, so into Aladdin's cave I looked, after a short while poking around I found a scythe, the old type that you see father time carrying around, it was a little dull and obviously had not been used much, a little more poking around and I found the stone to sharpen it with, so after a good deal of running the stone on the blade I finally got an edge, so back to the undergrowth I trotted, "whoosh" as I swung the huge blade into the tall weeds, and yes it cut like a dream so I persisted hacking away at what seemed an endless wall of weeds.

After a couple of hours it was time for the first display of the day so made my way down to the flying ground, Ray had taken down a lanner falcon to fly, the flying was superb, after answering a few questions from the public he came over to me and asked how I was getting along, my reply was something like, "bloody hard going" and like a true trooper he came to help me, when two people or more

45

tackle a job it seems to go quicker and become easier, if I remember correctly it took two or three days with the two of us working flat out to clear, once all the debris was raked into piles it was surprising how big the space was, Phillip came to see our progress and was very happy, timber was ordered from the local sawmill.

The next day we took the old green Renault estate, (which incidentally later that year I was to prang at the bottom of watery lane where it was quite narrow)with a trailer on the back over to the sawmill to collect the lumber.

On our return we un-loaded the wood and made a start on the framework, two weeks later a long row of smart new pens backed onto the hawk walk, we looked over them with pride, Ray and I agreed we deserved a cold beer, so off to the Yew Tree pub just up the road we went, sitting outside, life felt good, for the first time in years.

The routine in those days was after feeding round we all met up in the "Muzz" or museum and had coffee from the little machine in there I loved that coffee and so did everyone else, Phillip used to occasionally go up the wall how much coffee and creamer we were getting through, but it was nice, and we would find out what needed doing what school parties were coming round etc, on one particular morning Mima asked me to rake out the compartments on the hawk walk, these were mostly all the lanner falcons used for the displays and a good assortment of different species so the visitors could see birds up close and take photographs, so with rake in hand I headed off to the hawk walk to start work.

There were quite a few visitors that day, I think Dinah was taking round a school party, also a coach party and various families, so there I am in full view of the public raking out very professionally I might add each compartment, then it happened, a voice from behind me asked, "excuse me what do they eat dear", oh bugger, now I was on the spot, now I don't know where it came from but replied, "Scusey no engliase", someone behind her asked what did he say, the woman asking me the question replied to her "he doesn't speak English", "awww never mind" was the reply, yes I had actually stood there terrified to death and that had popped out of my mouth, as time went on of course I gained more confidence and actually took small school parties around and did flying demonstrations, I remember one school party in particular they were around 9 or 10 year olds about 20 if I remember right I was taking them around picking up various birds and Mozart and explaining a little about each type, I had just picked up a Redtail hawk, a female, and as I was going through my spiel I saw the sign oh oh I thought, as her tail lifted and before I could react and squirted out this huge mute-slice and it went all up this poor lads duffel coat which looked brand new!!, oh lord I thought this is going be trouble, but you know not one person had noticed!! Well yes only me and I felt awful, that poor lad must have gone home and had a right telling off for the mess on his coat, so if the parent of that young lad ever reads this please know I am terribly sorry, but I really couldn't have done much by the time I realized what was happening, (brief pause I have just realized my car keys are in my back pocket and I am sitting on them) and I am sure I passed the same woman later that day who asked me the question, whilst chattering away in English, she must of thought "wow he is a fast learner), days and weeks passed and as I said my confidence grew.

It was my birthday, that lunchtime I was called into the museum everyone was there, and Dinah presented me with a book as a gift, "Falconry in Arabia" by Mark Allen, the card that came with it Read, "Happy Birthday Chris, from everyone at the Centre", he has a wonderful memory your thinking?, I still have the book and the card!, after work that day Ray and his wife "Winnie", gave me a bottle of whiskey, which I was very grateful for "BUT" this was a bad idea on many levels, the main one being I did not drink often, Ray said he would meet up with me later and we would go up to the yew tree pub for a couple of drinks, after all it was my birthday.

The Yew tree was a nice little pub not too far away from the Centre, it had a pool table which Ray and I loved to play, him often than not thrashing me, the barman and owner was "Malcolm" a very welcoming host, a couple of games of pool and a few beers later we headed back, now I take full responsibility for what happened next, I said come on let's open your whiskey Ray was reluctant, "come on it's my birthday", so the whiskey was opened and we had one, then two...... the next thing poor Ray was hanging out the window being very ill indeed, at the sight of him being ill I joined in, there we were side by side hanging out of the window being ill, oh and that wasn't the worst of it, the bedroom I was in was high up (Dinah told me it was her sister Anna's old room with a lovely collection of 1970's music including an album by Steely Dan whom I still love to this day) and over looked the French doors where Phillip often stepped out in the evenings to smoke a cigar, so there we are hanging out of the top window, being ill all down the roof, oh crumbs Phillip stepped out with his cigar below us thank god for sloping roofs, and thank god he didn't look up or once again I would be in trouble I closed the window and helped Ray back to his room, I had the most perishing of looks off Winnie, a look that only a woman can give, I apologised, as best I could and sheepishly made my exit, I think it was three or four days before she spoke to me again, but all was forgiven, and things went back to normal.

One evening after work Phillip called me over and said, "would you like to come fishing?", without hesitation I replied, "yes please", "go and fetch the rods then", I knew where they were kept, so off I went to fetch them, oh lord, they were fly fishing rods, I had never done this before, my dad was a really keen course fisherman, the firm he worked for had a stretch of river at shipston-on-stour, and most weekends as a child we would go down there, and i learned the art of angling, but fly fishing, not a clue, so back with the rods I came i confessed i had never fly fished before, "oh don't worry Phillip said "I can show you, the rods were clipped along the roof of his silver Volvo estate and off we went, we arrived at some pools not too far away I jumped out opened the gate we drove through and parked up by the pools.

As well as he had taught me falconry Phillip taught me how to cast a fly line and within an hour or so I had got the hang of it, and I was fishing for trout!, first time out was fruitless for me but that was to be expected, a little later Phillip signalled to me and we headed back to the car, I believe he had caught two that day, on reaching home, as now it felt like home to me, I was shown how to smoke them and we later tucked into them for our evening meal and they were lovely.

Most days I would drive "Bill," Phillips wife into Newent, to do some grocery shopping, the Centre's runabout was a green beat up Peugeot estate, used for everything, collecting hawk food and general runabout duties, once I proved I could drive with competence I was allowed to drive Phillips silver Volvo estate, it was an automatic and like driving an arm chair, there Bill would visit the small supermarket and buy the daily provisions for lunch etc and anything household that was needed, on one particular occasion I was sent down to the little town as we had taken a sledge hammer into the iron mongers to have a new handle fitted, so I duly set off in the green Peugeot estate alone thankfully, I parked up and collected the newly refurbished sledge hammer and headed back, now anyone who knows the route well from Newent up to the Centre will know that once passed the secondary school there is a sort of "left and right bend in the lane around a barn, and just passed that point the lane narrows along a wall, as I reached this point a car was coming the opposite way down the lane, I pulled over and was slowing down the woman in the car coming in the opposite direction did the same, but the laws of physics tell us that two bodies cannot occupy the same space, and they didn't!, "crump", we collided alongside each other her wing mirror disappeared into the ether never to be seen again, I parked up and got out it was clear we were both shaken up, she said, "my husband is going to kill me", and I thought I know the feeling, so am I, the only damage to her car was the absent wing mirror which must have flew over the wall into a field of sheep, I wonder what the farmer thought when he found that?, I felt that sorry for her and I know I shouldn't have because it looked as if I was admitting guilt, and I believe we were 50/50 equal to blame, gave her the £30 I had been saving, we swapped registrations I told her where I was working and we carried on our separate ways, on my return I went straight to Phillip to confess what had happened.

He took it rather well, The words still come to mind, "oh bloody hell Chris", shortly followed by "are you ok", I said I was, I think I just pottered about for the rest of the day and I really felt I had let the side down, everyone said these things happen and not to worry about it, so I put it out of my mind, and carried on, 36 years later touch wood it is the only "bump" in a car I have had, oh and one parking ticket, don't get me started on that, or I will never finish this chapter.

The Centre was closed one day a week in those days, and on one particular closed days, we had John Noakes come down to do some filming, I had never met any celebrates before so it was all very new and exciting, we all gathered as usual that morning for coffee in the Muzz to await his arrival, a short while later in came a group of people from the BBC with sound equipment, cameras and a woman that held a clipboard and seemed to know everything that was going on, do they call them continuity people?, in amongst the host of people was John himself, I was very excited, but a little deflated as he had not brought with him his loyal companion "Shep", I didn't get a chance to speak to him as he was always surrounded by the BBC people and director sorting out what they were going to film, I believe it was for the series "Go with Noakes", which was a pretty big TV program of the day, the filming took most of the day although as with all things film wise the piece was only a few minutes long after editing etc, but still good exposure and advertising for the Centre.

8 ABDAB

That summer was long and warm and seemed to pass by very slowly, I had never 100% been a summer person, being fair haired as a child, my mother always kept me out of the sun, the winter was more preferable, there is nothing better than being tucked up in bed with the cold and rain firmly outside, and snow, was the best of all transforming the landscape into an icing sugar coated vision of serenity and beauty.

Tethered on the hawk walk was a female Lugger Falcon named "Abdab" we were not sure of her past, but as soon as she was approached she would scream, if anyone has ever heard a food imprint falcon scream for example, they will know exactly what this sounds like and how head splitting the sound is, Phillip thought me ready for the challenge, I think in all honesty no one there wanted to take her on, it was going to be difficult, and take a great deal of time, but Phillip assured me it was possible, here was my chance to prove myself and become part of the team.

I had never had a problem with the "Work Ethic", my dad being an ex-royal signaller, you had to be dead to be lying in bed past 8:00am, so I was always up early to get things done summer and winter, as a bit of a side note reading through this book it might appear that everything I touched I broke, or went wrong, NO, I am simply telling my story as it happened "warts and all".

I was to handle Abdab as much as possible with the view to stopping her screaming and me flying her for the public, during the daytime flying demonstrations, every evening after the daily maintenance and chores were complete, I would gently make into her, and pick her up, and carry her around the pathways and areas, gradually introducing her to other people, at first from many yards away, slowly and surely over the passing weeks the screaming became less and less, most of the time I sat with her for two or three hours after we closed to the public, gently talking to her, before I had even had any food myself, no wonder I was like a "stick", as the weeks slowly passed the screaming became less frequent, and I started her training, she was flying really well by now, just for me, and anyone else who happened to be in the flying area after hours, training there hawks, falcons too, she was far from ready to meet her public yet, I felt very proud of myself, and felt a great sense of achievement, as the days past she got stronger, more confident on the wing, the screaming had stopped completely, and she was deemed ready to meet the public.

It was decided I would fly her at first for very small groups of people, so on days where we had only a few people visit would be the time to pick her up and take her down to the flying area, which is in exactly the same spot to this day.

I actually made a visit back to the Centre earlier this year, first time in many years, after a long illness which I possibly may go into later in the book, mental health you see has a stigma very much attached to it still, Winston Churchill used to call it, his "Black Dog", his own reference to his depression, so I call mine the same, I love black dogs anyway especially Labradors, and I actually feel proud to be in the same company as Winston, if that man can lead a whole country through a world war, then I have a shot of writing this book, and finishing, while were on this I would like to say to anyone out there suffering in the same way, "there is light at the end of the tunnel", and "life is Good", it is also fine to get despondent and occasionally low, but it is not OK to give up, the people around us do love us, even though at times we may be in such a dark place we cannot see it, "never give up", If I can do it anyone can, you know some people sneered at me wanting to write this book, who does he think he is? etc, who am I?, I am the person that is as good as you, not better!, but as good as you, there is a quote by Mark Twain that sums it up quite well.

It was time for her public debut and to be honest, was I nervous, yes very, but I had rehearsed in my head many times how the display would go so, so picking her up off her block we headed off to the small weighing room at the top of the hawk walk, the bolt on the inside of the door firmly engaged behind me I proceeded to pop her on the scales, the scales we used at the time were the old huge white ones you often saw in butchers shops and were marked out for weighing sausages and meat, but with a slight modification to a perch became a very accurate method to determine a birds weight, crucial in understanding when a bird was keen enough to fly and respond well, with her weight duly noted and recorded on the large chalk board on the wall to the side down to the flying ground we set off passing the few visitors on the way down I proudly announced "we are about to fly a falcon, if you would like to follow me down", I had wanted to say this for so long, from in fact my very first visit to the Centre a few years earlier, the display didn't quite go how I had planned it, but still it went well enough for a a brand new display bird not used to so many people and to the sound of clapping, yes there was clapping, always a good measure of how well people enjoy something, my patter was not too bad with a few nervous stutters and mistakes, it is tricky trying to concentrate on swinging the lure well for your falcon and trying to talk, and fence off some of the questions thrown at you mid-flight by the onlookers, the public, thankfully there were little more than a handful, and as I remember they were very nice to us, I answered a few more questions from the people there present, standing amongst them and letting them take pictures and see her close up, "Abdabs" behaviour was impeccable, not so much as a peep from her, I was very proud indeed, we walked back up through the hawk walk this time with steam in my stride, repeated the process of weighing her, and noted down on the blackboard her weight, and how much food she had eaten, this is the way I was taught, and is a method I still use to this day, some things in falconry change but the basics still stay the same, many of the youngsters nowadays use grams, I still use pounds and ounces, and when ordering wood in feet and inches, I refuse to be metricated in these departments.

I continued with Abdabs manning and flying for some 6 weeks, gradually her flight abilities grew, she became stronger and more confident in the air, and we became very close partners, it is not like having a cat or a dog and is very hard to describe indeed.

When you are meeting people on a daily basis, you get to sort of feel when something is not right, on this particular day I had just flown Abdab and a group of three or four young men came up to me just as I was about to place her back on her block after weighing, they asked the usual kind of questions, and I believe thinking back were trying to come across as if they had no knowledge of falcons and falconry, which they clearly did, then one of them asked, "what weight does she fly at mate", the question kind of hit me as a little out of the ordinary, this was late in the morning, I think the 11:30 display, they moved on and I replaced Abdab on her block with a nice fresh Bath of clean water, just as a side note all birds are offered a bath of clean fresh water in the mornings, in case they want one, it is a bit late when you start to fly or hunt your bird and decide to go off in search of water for a bath, it can totally ruin your day and at worst result in a lost hawk.

What followed next none of us were ready for, or even expected, we had just closed around 5:30, we were all doing various things feeding around the birds, putting baths away, all of a sudden all of the alarms had sprung into life, I was down by the house, we all ran and gathered in the hawk walk and began to look around at this point it was not clear if the system had been tripped accidental as we made our way down the hawk walk the two gates either side that led down into the aviary area were stuck, I shouted "I can't get the gate open", then we realized why, they had both been wired shut with what looked like coat hanger wire, we got them open and went through there was no sign of anyone, some were still in the hawk walk, as I made my way back up I saw everyone gathered around where the display falcons were tethered, I looked into the compartment where I had placed Abdab, her leash had been cut at the base of the block, and she was gone, as I write I can feel the tears in my eyes still now to this day, I don't remember much else as I ran and sat on the bench outside the little museum, I was heartbroken, angry all at the same time, and pretty much inconsolable, some bastard had taken her how bloody dare they I had put my heart and soul and everything I had inside me into that bird, I was so furious and upset, the police were telephoned, and arrived while we searched the surrounding area again and looked for any clues, but they were long gone, I gave a statement, and best I could a description to the police about the group of guys earlier in the day and gave as best I can, but I do have to say, it may not have been them at all, all I will say is that my instincts to this day about people are rarely wrong, and whoever did steal her away from me, and the Centre, I hope they see this book, and read this section, and see how much damage and hurt they caused in there moment of greed and grasping desire, although people that do this sort of thing rarely have a conscience in my experience anyway, one can only hope they eventually do.

The next day felt very empty indeed to me, I had now lost some purpose, I was still very shocked upset and deflated, but as you do you pick yourself up and carry on, this is definitely the best medicine, otherwise these criminals win, the police came back, they were more than helpful, they agreed to come back that night with night vision equipment, we had sort of figured out the route they had taken and plans were made to make camp in a disused sheep shelter made of corrugated tin sheets in an adjacent field, while it was still light we settled ourselves down in the shelter it was remarkably comfy and all the surveillance gear was set up, night time fell and the night vision equipment was turned on, I had never seen this sort of equipment before it certainly would have shown us if anyone dare come back they would have had a burly policeman to deal with, the night passed without event and as daylight crept on, we decided to go back and grab an hour or so of sleep before the working day began, we bid farewell to our police companion and headed off to try and sleep, if I remember correctly they came back a few nights but when it was obvious the thieves were not returning the police reluctantly decided to call the surveillance a day, we upgraded the security significantly.

It was a good two weeks before I came back out of my shell, and to this day I still miss that falcon, I can only hope for her sake she led a happy and fruitful existence.

Something exciting and a totally new experience was to come along, the BBC had been in touch and we were tasked to film a piece for a TV program for the life of me I cannot remember but the show featured animals and a falcon, so the day arrived, I was to assist Mima that day and happily accepted the challenge, the BBC film crew arrived with the most amazing soft top American car I had ever seen, the director told me it was all they could get for what was needed, which would soon become apparent so Mima, me and a Lanner falcon piled into the various cars and headed off to a local small airport.

On arrival we were directed to a small airstrip that permission had been gained to use, the shot they were after was a falcon following camera, and to do this Mima was to kneel on the back seat of this fabulous American car, the car would pull away with Mima swinging the lure, and at the right moment I was to release the bird she would chase the lure and the shot was in the can as they say, well in theory that was the idea, on the first take we all took our positions, Mima kneeling centrally on the back seat facing backwards, with the cameraman and me standing on the airstrip waiting for the signal to release the bird, someone from the group shouted "action", and at that moment the driver of the American car shot off at full speed, puffs of smoke from the back tires, oh dear the driver had over-estimated the speed of the bird by about 100 miles an hour, and if I had of released she definitely would not have kept up with the car, how Mima kept her balance I will never know!, the air turned slightly blue there were a few giggles at the driver, I'm sure he just wanted to see how powerful the car was, we lined up the shot again for another try, things went better, we did a few more as we all settled into the routine, they had captured the shot they needed, I think we were treated to lunch, and back to the Centre we headed, it certainly was a fun day, I do not think I will ever forget how fast the driver pulled away on that first take, leaving us all coughing in the wake, funny indeed.

9 PINKY

Our fishing trips continued and I gradually got more proficient at casting and placing the fly where I had seen a fish rise, I remember the very first time I caught a trout, because the rods are so light and rainbow trout have a lot of fight in them it was all very exciting and I was definitely hooked, Phillip had been flying his female Harris hawk called "Pinky", and he very kindly allowed me to take her flying after the day's work was done, in those days it was possible to cross the road in front of the Centre and explore the fields opposite, Pinky was a dream to fly I had never experienced the fun of flying a Harris hawk before, in point of fact Pinky was the first Harris hawk I had ever seen, she had a lovely demeanour and was a pleasure to take out, she would happily follow along, or sit still on the fist depending on the situation, I continued to take her out most evenings, and we both got very fit in the process, I think I weighed around 10 1/2 stone at that time, and being six feet tall I looked like a strip of wind.

After lunch one day I was doing some odd jobs in the Hawk Walk, Phillip came through the gate that led down to the house, beckoned me over and said, "Come and see", so back through the gate and down to the tiny lawn by the house, there sat on a bow perch was a really nice looking hawk in immature plumage, "do you know what it is"?, Phillip asked, I took one more look to make double sure, "I think it is a young male common buzzard" was the reply, "what do you think of him?", I said something like "he is in good condition, and yes I like him", "Well he is yours", I was totally taken by surprise and had a job to hold back my emotions, my falconry hero, so to speak, mentor and employer who suffered me had bought me a hawk, I managed to get out the words "thank you", he said "now get him going".

Over the next couple of weeks, his training progressed well, although in the wild common buzzards can be lazy hunters, I was very surprised how keen "Mikey" was yes I had given him a name, I think Winnie came out with a saying, or catch phrase from some American TV program of the day, "Mikey Likes It" so the name just kind of stuck.

By the time his training was complete the dark nights had begun to draw in and the Centre took on a feeling of calm and a stillness that even today I can remember, visitors were becoming less and less as the weather turned wet, everything seemed to step down a gear, It was time to go "a hunting", as the days were short and daylight was at a premium to me it made more sense to take my little buzzard across the road, we had a few other places reasonably nearby, but as this would involve a car journey to take him over the road would give me precious more light to fly him, so across the road I went, hopped over the fence as 20 odd year olds do, "note to self", do not hop over fences at my age.

I was carrying him on my gloved hand "Fist" whilst tapping along the hedge with a long stick, maybe it was the wet weather or just one of those days but we saw nothing, so I thought while I am here I may as well call him a few times, and he came back instantly each time, we were about half a mile into our walk when it started to light drizzle, I had just put Mikey into a tree and was tapping the hedge up to him in the hope of making something run out underneath him, when all of a sudden he dropped out of the tree on the other side of the hedge, then came the "waaak waak waak", this sound was all too familiar to me it was a crow, if I had a companion with me I'm sure they would have been very impressed, I ran around the other side and there was Mikey sitting and holding on tight to his dinner, I made my way in and assisted as falconers do, as we have a responsibility to the quarry we hunt, after a while I swapped his prey for a juicy piece of beef and slipped the crow into my bag, the weather now had gotten worse, and we made our way back, walking home in the rain with your first catch with your new hawk is a feeling that you never lose well for me anyway, I couldn't wait to get back to show Phillip, I was so proud, I was so proud in fact that I lost all sense of etiquette went striding into the house, Hawk still on first into the kitchen where Phillip, Bill, and a few others were, I burst in, "look at what we caught", and slapped the dead crow down on Bill's kitchen table, the moment I did this I had that sinking feeling, and the thought you shouldn't have done that, Bill went ballistic, "get that bloody thing off my table, take it out", I looked at Phillip he didn't say much, I could see he understood the situation and told me to take it out, I was soaked to the skin, I fed and sorted out Mikey, at supper that evening there were a few giggles going around the table, I went and apologized to Bill later that evening, she just smiled, I sat down at the kitchen table and stayed and chatted a while, Bill had a little tape machine in the kitchen and loved to listen to Edith Piaf recordings, it was like having a mother to talk to again something I so dearly missed.

Halloween was close and we, that is Dinah, Ray, Winnie, Fergus, myself and Alice who lived on the fruit farm next door to the Centre, which was an amazing place to visit the farm as I remember it, sloped down away from watery lane, down the hill to the bottom, in the summer it was the most breathtaking view with all the neat rows of fruit trees running top to bottom it was truly inspiring, even more so because Alice's dad did it all himself, he was a spitfire pilot during WW2, and a very interesting man to talk to indeed, we all decided we were going to celebrate Halloween by getting dressed up and go round a few of the pubs in and around Newent, Alice came up with the Idea and said she would make some Damson Vodka, as we still had a few weeks to go this should be ready for drinking by then, so we all set about making costumes after the daily duties had been performed, some of us bought masks and others made them.

Finally the day arrived and we all met up in the sitting room, we had a good laugh at each other as we hadn't seen any part of each other's costumes until the day, we tried some of Alice's damson vodka, then tried it again to make sure it was ok, and off we went in the now mended green Peugeot estate, and I didn't drive it oh no, I was taking no chances, after we had visited a couple of pubs I began to realize we had been that excited putting our outfits together, making them look as realistic as possible, I was carrying around with me a huge felling Axe that we used to cut the logs for the house!, can you imagine that happening these days, you would probably be surrounded by a police armed response unit and handcuffed, I expressed my concerns to the others, and after a few more pubs I had forgotten about it, and we headed home, just to check the damson vodka was still OK, we had another.

Between Halloween and bonfire night we had a visitor to the Centre, a Frenchman, sadly I cannot remember his name, I should be able to as I am part French myself!, I believe he had made the trip from France to specifically visit the Centre, he was full of life always laughing, waving his arms around in an excited fashion a really fun chap, as we were closed to the public by then the place was very quiet, he was shown around, once that was done Phillip tasked me with taking him fishing, so I grabbed the rods and equipment and we made our way out to his car you know the little French hatch backs of the time, I had to hold the rods out of the window alongside of the car as of course he didn't have those useful little rod clips that fastened to the rain guttering lip on a car roof, now let me tell you holding rods out of a car window when it is cold is no mean feat, especially when you have a full of life Frenchman who is used to driving on the other side of the road and drives at speed everywhere, I thought my hand would freeze up and drop off, once again breaking something and getting into trouble, oh, and as soon as we headed off in his car I realized why he was in such a good mood and very animated, there was a clinking from under both our seats and the back seat foot well, it was FULL of bottles of wine, yes, he was pissed!!.

We somehow managed to arrive at the fishing pools, we setup the rods and began to fish, but the best was yet to come, he cracked open a bottle of red wine, well the sun was over the yardarm as they say so I had some, he even had wine glasses in the glove box of the car, how organized I remember thinking, now drinking red wine with a Frenchman that has brought red wine from France you know it is going to be good, and it was, I wish I could remember the names on the labels but after 34 odd years, no chance, I can't remember them from last week, so we set about demolishing that bottle and another one, I decided as I hadn't caught a fish from the side of the pool I would move onto the little jetty, I walked over cast in looked down, and what I saw nearly took me off balance, I called my happy companion over, "look I said" it is a body, a human body at the bottom of the pool, the water there was a few feet deep he went off, arms in the air, rod in the water, isn't it funny how you can still make out swear words even in a foreign language, I was mortified but in control, well somebody had to be, after the initial shock had worn off we moved closer it was a full size human skeleton, "is it real" my companion asked I'm not sure I said, so we opened another bottle of red wine to calm ourselves down, so we fished it out with a landing net and sure enough it was a full size human skeleton the type you often see in hospitals as a teaching aid, so we dragged it out on the jetty so it could dry off a bit, we sat there drinking our wine for a while, Once dry we carried back the skeleton to the car, and promptly sat him in the passenger seat me in the back, we had some funny looks on the way back I can tell you, on arrival we regaled our story, both this time in an animated fashion to hoots of laughter, we discovered a couple of days later that it had been a Halloween prank by some medical students that had "borrowed" the skeleton and placed it in the trout pool as a student's prank, they collected it later that week.

As the year grew older Ray and Winnie set off back home to America, this was the last time I was to see them both, goodbyes were said and I was left on my own, I think Mima and I shared the feeding round, the winters seemed much colder then, very odd as the older I have got the more tolerance I seem to have to the cold, not sure if this is a good or bad thing, I suppose if my fingers ever drop off with frost bite it is a bad thing, Christmas was almost upon us and I was due to return home for a couple of weeks, which I have to confess I wasn't looking forward too, a few weeks earlier I had to take a video recorder for Phillip to exchange it, and it was a stone's throw from Tamworth, and I thought I will call in and see my Dad, so off I set in the Peugeot again up the M50, M5 M42 after exchanging the video I headed for Tamworth not knowing what reception I would get.

I pulled up at the house and walked in the back door as I normally would the house was warm and there was a kettle boiling I shouted "hello Dad!", nothing, I shouted again a little louder and he said Chris is that you? I said yes, just having a shave came the reply but he flew down the stairs and hugged me, I had never seen such emotion from him before he said, great to see you son, and I replied something like it is good to be here, we sat and chatted for about an hour before he was due to go on night shift, he asked if I was home to stay I explained about exchanging the video and said let us see what the new year brings, I headed back to Newent feeling a lot better, relieved, at calling in at home, now I knew where I stood, I was welcome back anytime so although I had broken the ice with dad I still had to put up with his new girlfriends horrid spoiled children and her, it made me angry the way they soaked money off him, not that I wanted things for myself but the fact he was a very generous man and they took advantage of him at every opportunity, and nothing I seemed to say or do would dissuade him otherwise, I suppose the old saying "love is blind" really is true but I'm sure it wasn't love on her side just an easy meal ticket... baa humbug.

As I remember Phillip let me take the old green Peugeot estate home that Christmas as it saved on train and bus fares for me, and it would not be needed at the centre over the festive and New Year period.

10 SPARROWHAWKS

I could not think of sitting down to write a book without including the sparrowhawk, this bird has always been kind of magical for me, some of my best memories are of flying these wonderful little hawks that bring so much pleasure and delight to me.

Up until this time of writing I have successfully flown, hunted and released several female and male sparrowhawks, the males are the "Musket" and the females referred to as "Spars", there is a mixed woodland very close to where I live and have spent many hours observing them at their nest site when I was younger we used to camp up in the woods so we could get up early to watch them and maybe even catch a glimpse of the young as they grew and ventured out of the nest, so much fun can be had with these amazing little hawks, but not for the beginner.

I can remember on one occasion when I was still working in the pop factory a few of my friends and I decided we were going to camp in the wood for the weekend, we planned the "expedition" weeks in advance and made sure we had all the necessities teenage lads would need to go camping, torches, matches for lighting a fire and about six tins of baked beans each, now let me tell you if you live on a diet of baked beans for a couple of days you begin to look like a bake bean and "hmm mm" dare I say "pass" them too, we were due to set off when I finished work on the evening, I had taken my rucksack all packed up with me that Friday morning and left it in the locker room at work, by the time I had finished and everyone had arrived to meet me it was getting on not yet dusk but not far off, we were walking on foot it was a couple of miles or so to the woods, we passed the walk by drinking cans of pop I had bought from the staff shop, you could buy a whole pack of 24 cans for about £2:00 which was pretty good, anyway we finally arrived at the woods and it was getting pretty dark one of the lads said "follow me" I know the way, and we followed along, oh here is a good tip, don't pack torches at the bottom of rucksacks as you can't find them, anyway our new found leader was that confident he knew the way we followed on till we found a clearing with beautiful short grass "he said here is a good place" and we all had to agree, it is quite rare to find flat ground with short grass to camp on in the middle of a hilly mixed woodland, so we sat about putting up our tents, we were so tired after the walk that we didn't bother with food the idea was to get up early the next day and heat up our beans, so after some banter and the usual trumping contest we all fell asleep, now the funny thing with camping I have found, well for me anyway is that as soon as its light and the tent fills with light, "Bing" I'm awake, so after a few moments of gathering where I actually was I unzipped my sleeping bag, then the tent door, aren't tent zips noisy?, you feel like you are going to wake the whole village up by unzipping then re zipping the door up, so here is the scene, me standing outside the tent in my underpants and socks, not a pretty sight I can tell you "watering the horses", if you follow me?, looking around, admiring the lovely flat area still watering the horse I turned round to go back in my tent "oh bullocks, there, right in front of me was what we called "the Wood house", it was a property near the edge of the wood owned at the time by I believe a Barrister, and the bloody grass was so short, flat and well-kept because it was his lawn, we had only stumbled onto it in the dark without realizing and were camped about 100 or so feet from his French windows, and I had just "watered my horse", on his lawn!!, as quickly and quietly as I could I woke the others, thank god it was summer time and first light was stupid o'clock early, you have never seen a group of lads move so swift and quiet to remove three, two man tents in your life, we ran further into the wood collapsing in a heap of laughter, it was indeed our lucky day, we left no mess behind us so hopefully he never knew, but the racket we made when setting up, it is a wonder we didn't wake anyone or maybe they were out for the evening.

Anyway we set up camp at the new location and decided to cook breakfast and we heated up our beans still chortling over what had happened, after breakfast the other lads went ferreting, we agreed a time to meet back at the camp, no mobile phones in them days it was all done by the watch, whilst I headed off to find the spars nest.

I headed to an area at the top of the woods which was a few acres of pine trees, I figured this was the best place if I was going to find sparrowhawks, so I carefully entered, and sat down by an old fallen pine tree which made a perfect vantage point to observe any activity high up in the canopy, I had been here many times before and new the layout of the wood pretty well, except after dark without torches it seems!!, so I sat down and to listen, before too long I heard that familiar sound, I smiled to myself, I think I must have sat there most of the day watching those sparrowhawks, eyes glued to the canopy through binoculars, a very peaceful and pleasant way to spend a summer day on a Saturday we met up back at the campsite around tea time, well my belly said it was teatime, the other lads returned with a couple of rabbits, wonderful, meat for tea, there is nothing more tasty than fresh rabbit cooked on sticks by an open fire, we were the Ray Mears and Bear Grylls of our time, in fact there was a popular TV program on at the time called "Grizzly Adams" he was our hero and instead of a big old grizzly bear called Ben we had ferrets, we set about skinning and jointing up the the rabbits, feeding the ferrets first as they had provided us with this lovely meal, I didn't feed them, I tried that once a few years previously a lad down our street used to keep ferrets, not very well, not handled much etc, one latched onto my finger and I never forgot it, and to this day I will not have one, I'm sure I would catch more rabbits if I did have one, but the size of the bag was never foremost in my mind, but being outside, in the countryside with a trained hawk, chasing quarry is, we sat and munched on the rabbit with beans, sitting around the fire as it grew dark drinking our coke cans, life really doesn't get much better than that!, fresh air always seems to have the same effect on me we were all sleepy and headed off to our tents, we had arranged them in a circle around the fire, it was quite nice laying there with the tent door open, watching the flames flickering and fading into glowing embers, lovely way to drift off.

The next morning I was awake at first light, I heard movement in the tent next door "ziiiiip" as the door opened and closed, a voice came, "I'm off to the village to get milk won't be long,

OK I replied then I thought "milk" it is about 4:30 or there about the shop won't be open, oh well I thought, its Sunday morning I'm going lay here a bit, have you ever noticed when camping, even in summer everything seems to feel damp?, I have to admit these days I loathe camping and much prefer a proper bed, a couple of hours passed and I heard footsteps through the bracken outside a voice, I'm back I hurriedly dressed and crawled out, "I got some things, I made some remark about it was still too early for the shop to open, out of the rucksack came 3 pints of milk, a packet of bacon, half a dozen eggs and some potatoes, "where the bloody hell you had these from, erm came the reply, "I saw the milkman, waited for him to leave then sort of helped myself, he had only gone and took the provisions off the doorsteps down in the village, that's it I said the police will be up here now, at all this commotion the others awoke and fell about laughing, it's not funny I said its stealing, I wasn't happy, but I did drink the milk and eat the bacon and eggs, that poor milkman I bet he got in all sorts of bother with the villagers over that, after our meal the others decided they had enough and packed up their gear said there farewells and headed home leaving me there alone which was fine as I have always enjoyed my own company even to this day, I packed up my tent, sleeping bag and gear, and headed off back to the sparrowhawk wood, I stopped there for a few hours then headed off back home, and had a few Hours sleep in a proper bed.

I had already trained one female sparrowhawk by this point, flown her for a season, then passed her onto a friend when work commitments got in the way, it is not fair to keep a bird tethered to a bow perch, as many did in those days when you have to work and cannot fly them, any birds I have these days are all "free lofted" which basically means they are loose in a pen with clean water and various perches, in fact my male Harris hawk at the time of writing is free lofted in his pen and even has a heater tube under one shelf perch where he can choose to sit if the nights get really frosty, frost rises about a yard or so above ground level so he has enough perches above this level to get out of the way of it, oh and the heater tube is on a timer too so I do not have to worry about forgetting to turn it on in case of a frost, or the weather forecasters fail to warn us of a heavy frost, we all know how accurate weather forecasts can be don't we?.

As time passed still more sparrowhawks came to live with us, most being hunted and released, passed onto friends and of course on occasion they died, the more you fly a particular bird the more you know about its well-being and usually you can spot if they look a bit under the weather, their general demeanour can tell you a lot about a birds health that day, in fact Phillip taught us this to look at your bird every morning, which I still do to this day every day!, it is a quick way of making sure everything is well, of course there are accidents that no one can foresee, at the time of writing a friend of mine left her sparrowhawk feeding on a quail and it choked on a bone, these things happen, fact of life but there is no excuse for not taking a sick bird to the vets, costs should never be a factor, as was drummed into me if you cannot afford a vet then don't get a bird, these days you can get Insurance on Birds of prey the same as you can get on cats and dogs, and my little Harris hawk costs me £4 and a few odd coppers a month to keep insurance, priceless when you think about it, I mean a packet of cigarettes are around £8, so it is a no brainer.

One particular little male sparrowhawk, a Musket stands out in my mind particularly, the area I live most people know I keep birds so there is always something turning up on the doorstep, it was over a Christmas period so I was off work and a knock came at the door, it was an old school friend carrying a small cardboard box, apparently this bird had got stuck in some old pea netting that had not been taking down at the end of the vegetable growing season and this poor little chap had got himself tangled, he said I have no idea what bird it is, as I had no birds of my own at that time I agreed to take it in and try and nurse it back to health, I took the cardboard box up the garden, at the time I had a shed attached to an 18ft long flight inside the shed were a couple of night quarter boxes where birds could be put out of the cold or if I had a sick bird, a small freezer, scales and a radio, I carefully placed the box onto the work surface making sure the shed door was bolted securely behind me as you never know what if anything will explode from the box, I slowly and as quietly as I could opened the top and there to my astonishment and utter delight sitting in the corner of the box was a little musket resplendent in his adult plumage, his chest was the deepest orange colour and looked almost rusty, his back was a very dark slate grey, and his little piercing yellow eyes were almost mesmerizing, I could tell by his general look that he was low in condition and very hungry indeed kind of like how we get when we haven't eaten all weak and listless, I carefully closed the lid, turned on the tube heater that I had in the shed just to bring the temperature up a bit, I had hawk food in the freezer, quail in those days was hard to get hold of if at all, so I set about thawing out some beef, for him, I had spent a lot of time with the vets that used to come to the Centre, and always made a point of trying to be there when the vet was called in to treat a sick bird or if an injured bird had been brought in, and learn as much as I could, this should never be a replacement for professional veterinarian care, but sometimes in an emergency situation you have to act fast, or indeed if it is out of hours, anyhow back to the little musket, I had thawed out some beef and cut it into peanut sized pieces and had it soaking in a glucose saline solution, I took the little chap out carefully, now normally a wild bird would be quite active and not like being handled at all but he was as quiet as a mouse, and popped him on my lap, I picked up a piece of the soaking meat and gently teased it around his beak, hopefully irritating him enough to open his mouth and take it, after a little coaxing he took it, and just lay there with it in his mouth as if to say "well I've got it what do you want me to do with it now?, I held my breath, and he swallowed the tiny piece of meat down, the next one he took with no trouble at all and I thought this looks promising, the muskets have a really tiny body weight, one I flew was around 6 1/2 oz so if the weather is cold and they have not eaten they can go downhill pretty fast, also glucose saline can be given subcutaneously to rehydrate them, which I did on this occasion as well as I felt he needed that little boost, I carried on feeding him the same way throughout the night and by morning he was standing upright and looking much like a soldier on parade, after the Sargent major had said "ateeeeeeenshun!", he stayed with me for about a week getting stronger each day, I was so tempted to keep him and fly him, he was a little "pip".

Finally the day came for me to release him and I have to observe how calm he was around people and not in the least worried I wondered if he had been trained before?, he had no ring on his leg so I had no way of telling, I was to release him from my back garden, as this is the area he was found this was the right thing to do, now what follows is 100% true and still amazes me to this day when I think about it, I released him and he flew onto the fence, he sat there for a good 5 minutes looking around surveying the area, he then took off and flew down towards where he had been found, I rushed out of the gate onto the grassed area at the back in order to watch him fly off into the distance and what followed I still can't believe, he flew some 100/120 yards, threw up in a vertical climb, then flipped over as only a spar can do, and was flying straight towards me at head height, I stood frozen in wonder to the spot as this little bird flew straight at me, as he passed over my head he jinked and his little wing brushed the top of my head as if to say "thank you", I turned and watched him fly into the distance, I was flat gob smacked, and it took some time to sink in at what had just happened, I used to keep an eye open for him especially in winter I always imagined he would pop by to say hello, but never did see him again, it left me with a deep feeling of satisfaction and I went back inside a happy bunny.

Some months passed and I got a phone call one evening from a friend, who told me a woman had just telephoned him in tears as her kestrel had gone of its legs, I agreed to go and take a look at her bird as it was out of hours for the vets, which should be everyone's first port of call always, and she sounded pretty desperate, a short time past and my friend picked me up in his car and drove me to her home, we were shown into the front room of a small terraced house which appeared to be an old miners cottage on the edge of some fields, , she hurriedly ushered us into the room where a cardboard box was sitting on the table, inside was a towel and laying on it was the prettiest little female kestrel named "Callie", she looked very poorly indeed slow labored breathing, and very listless, very low in condition, I had taken some glucose saline with me and gave her a good dose under the skin, I said to the dreadfully upset woman, "I think it best I take her home with me", I could tell it was going to be a long night ahead, she agreed, and we headed back to my home.

I set about cutting some tiny pieces of beef up and soaking them in the glucose saline solution, at first having to hand feed the poor little girl, encouraging her to swallow the tiny morsels, after she was able to swallow a couple of the tiny pieces I knew I was in with a chance.

I kept her in the tiny cardboard box, by the hot water tank where it was nice and warm, and every hour I fed her a few more pieces of beef, as the night drew on she slowly got stronger wiggling around and sitting on her front, with her little black eyes slowly closing as I watched her nodding in and out of sleep, by morning she was sitting up and taking the tiny pieces of meat from me, I telephoned the woman who's name escapes me I'm sorry, and told her the good news, I said "she is sitting up and eating and I think she will be fine", I relayed to her, as you would expect she was over the moon, as she was convinced she had lost her, it was a very close call indeed, she agreed that I kept her for another couple of days, I fed her as much as she would eat, she was an absolute little poppet, and it felt good to be able to help someone, we returned her back to her owner who was beside herself with delight, I think I shed a tear or too as well, and little Callie went on to give many more years of pleasure to her owner, I went back home and slept for a few hours, feeling content.

Around this time I joined the BFC (The British Falconers Club) up until this point I had always been a solitary person and much preferred my own company, hunting with a hawk to me was always a very personnel thing, and I can count on the fingers of two hands the times I have been out "Hawking" with others, I do not like it, and never will, I was persuaded to join by a friend as it was the "right thing to do" for the sport at the time and it was when hunting with hawks was under threat so as a good citizen and passionate about the sport it was my duty to stand with my hawking brothers and sisters, just after joining there was to be a field meet quite close to me , so I went along, we had a wonderful day, one of the chaps female Harris hawks even caught a wild mink!, I got chatting to one chap and became friends with, and he lived quite close to me around half a mile away, at the time I wasn't flying any birds, he invited me round to see his small collection, he had a breeding pair of Harris hawks that he had not long put together, and he was flying a male Harris named "Charlie", it was quite obvious me and Charlie were going to become friends, he had such a personality and if it was ever possible to click with a hawk, we "clicked", the job I was working allowed me two days off a week, and with rearing a young family of my own we had only just been able to afford a car, it was a second hand beige coloured Ford Fiesta, and was a good little runabout, my new found friend made a very kind offer, he said that anytime I wanted to fly Charlie I could, brilliant I thought, I could even take him and fly him on his permission ground, he lived in a row of terraced houses with huge gardens to the rear, I would park up the little fiesta go up the side entry through his gate into the garden pick up Charlie and take him to the car, I used to drop down the back seats and had a sort of portable bow perch which he used to hop onto, and love to look out the window on the way to where we flew, you get some funny looks off people with a big hawk sitting on a bow perch or even a car perch which fitted over the back of an upright seat so the bird could happily sit there on the top taking stock, nowadays most use a plastic transit box I know they make a lot more sense!, he would sit there quite happily whilst I took off my glove closed the tailgate and set about our journey, when we arrived my routine which is pretty much the same as it is today, I would first prepare the transmitter and check it was working ok, put on my hawking bag that contained a piece of beef and several smaller pieces to offer as little rewards as we went around the fields, and then a long beating stick some 4 feet long shoved through my belt at the back, this done, he would then hop onto the glove, whilst I would fit the tiny transmitter onto his tail, "Telemetry" as we call it is a vital piece of kit used by pretty much everyone these days, and is within reach of all pockets, the transmitter has a sort of spring clip that attaches to a tiny tube crimped onto the birds tail feather or "deck" feather, the deck feather being one of two middle of the tail feather which are the most straight if you like as they are central, the tube is crimped over the hollow feather shaft, which causes no harm or pain to the bird in the slightest as it is hollow and exterior to the body, you kind of squeeze the clip together slide it up the tube and it springs open and the little tags on the end spring out and into the tube and it is the reverse to take it off, I always choose the deck feather closest to me when the hawk is sitting on the glove, makes it a tiny bit easier, well for me anyway, the other part of the system is a receiver with a built in Ariel that is directional and should your bird catch something in the distance which often happens as they chase things and land with

it in thick cover you can recover the bird quite quickly, oh, and it helps if you can run, so this for me is the very first thing and last thing that comes off when flying, and as I said there is no real excuse not to use them, Charlie was pretty good at catching rabbits and we had immense fun together, his owner also had a cottage in wales and spent his time between the two homes so I was taking him out flying quite a lot, and I was thinking this is the next bird I want it would suit my situation perfectly.

Simon, one of the three musketeers had recently started working for the Falconry Centre and he lived in a small flat at the Centre, so any holidays I had I would go down and spend a few days or a week there, and I would help out, he made the most delicious chilli, and would eat it most evenings we had some good times there, it was nice to see old faces and friends.

On one visit Mima knew I was without a hawk, She had a coopers hawk there a female that was getting on a little and I was asked if I would like to take her and fly her so "Diana" came to stay, by this time my friend had sold his cottage in wales and was pretty much flying Charlie full time so everything sort of fell right into place.

I have to say Diana was a joy to get going and I was to have many happy expeditions with her.

A girl where I worked had married a farmer and they lived in a small village not too far from me I asked what would be the chances of flying my little hawk up there, and the answer came back "come and fly whenever you like", so I did every chance I got they were pig farmers and had a pig breeding unit set up but the land they had was huge, I picked a time when I knew my work colleague would be there and I went up, I was shown and pointed out all the fields I could go in, the farm sort of sloped down towards a small river at the bottom so plenty of room for Diana to stretch her wings, there was also a pond on there with moorhen's swimming about, we had a lot of fun chasing those, but on one occasion I was to be once more gob smacked, my day off used to be Thursdays back then and the expedition was planned I had got her weight just right and she was keen, the weight is pretty crucial in hunting birds, but as an analogy it is like me saying to someone here is a lovely roast dinner, then after they had eaten it and were well fed and content saying would you nip round the shop for me please?, or saying to someone if you nip round the shop for me I will have a lovely roast dinner for you when you return, you are more likely to want to go with the promise of a nice meal at the end of it experienced falconers will already know this but feel it necessary to explain the rudiments of how we encourage our hawks to work with us.

On this particular day I had just finished kitting up, transmitter fitted bag and stick slipped through belt, oh what you also learn is "sods law", if it can happen it will happen so from the moment I locked the car and return to open it I have my bird on the gloved fist ready to slip as it is quite possible to walk around the fields and then get back to near where you park the car than a rabbit or pheasant will get up and you have already re-fitted the mews Jesse's swivel and leash and cannot take the slip, anyhow I had Diana on my fist ready to go, locked the car and quietly entered the largest field which sloped away downhill to the river at the bottom, as soon as I entered a hare got up and started running some 25 or so yards away a fraction of a second before I saw it Diana saw it, and she was off like a shot after it, the hare ran downhill away from me but Diana was hard on its tail, she was quite fit as she was flown most days, now if you've ever seen the size of a coopers hawk to a hare you will understand how funny what I am about to tell you, she grabbed the hare at the nape of the neck on the back and was riding on this hare like a tiny jockey, I was tearing down the field after them, she had no chance of bringing it down, they carried on for another ten yards or so before the Hare kicked her off before disappearing through a hedge and away, when I got to Diana she was laying on her back feet in the air panting, I said something like "are OK old girl", like she could answer me, I could see she was fine just her pride was hurt, that image has stuck in my mind ever since, Diana stayed with me for another couple of years before her age took her away from me, and she now resides buried on my property with some wonderful memories that thankfully time has kept warm, and fresh and dear to me, Diana was a little star.

11 WOODBINE

After Diana had gone it once again left a gaping hole in my free time, and again my thoughts turned towards a male Harris hawk, they fascinated me almost as much as the sparrowhawk, they were bright and were thinkers and had their own little characters, each one different, and I liked this.

I was still making trips down to visit Simon helping out at the Centre when I had time off from work and when my wife had nothing for me to paint or do around the house, hiding the paint brushes can help slightly, on one visit I asked Mima about a Harris and expressed my desire to own and fly a male, a month or so later I had a phone call, they had a male that was surplus to requirements and needed a new good home, at the time somewhere in the early to mid-1980's the price of these birds were still very high, I was working for a high street electrical outlet and they were an awful company driven by profit and had a "carrot and stick" method of treating there staff with always the threat of the sack, or "there are plenty more people out there that would jump in your shoes" attitude, we were poorly paid and treated like muck, in point of fact we were that poorly paid I showed a wage slip several years later where I got the response, "well you are going to find it tough, if you've been earning that much a week!!", when Pointed out that the wage slip was for a "monthly" salary she said, I feel very sorry for you, there idea of paying overtime was if you worked all day on a Sunday putting in the stores Christmas promotion they bought you a burger meal and thought they were being over generous in doing that, let me tell you when your earning £230 a month have a family to keep etc a bloody burger meal isn't even a joke, I can remember on one occasion I actually caught a thief who had broken into a woman's car, stolen a credit card from her purse, came into the shop and purchased £3000 worth of electrical goods and because of me thinking there was something wrong did a check and the police came in and arrested them, I got a thank you letter from the board of directors thanking me for my swift action, I turned round and said "well that is lovely but I can't take this letter and spend it in Sainsbury's can I?", and do you know what?, they gave me a written warning for saying it too, they were horrid, the way they treated us lead to me ultimately having a nervous breakdown, anyhow I've gone off track a bit, so the price of a male Harris was four months wages to me at the time, and personally I think they still should be the same, luckily a few years before I had taken out an endowment policy, where you pay a few pounds a month then after ten years you cash it in for a chunk of cash, after some hand wringing and a chat with my wife I approached the co-op and asked for a cash in figure I can remember the insurance agent coming out to the house to try and talk me out of cashing it in, but I was set on my goal, and trying to convince another salesman into doing something or not as was the case he was on a loser from the moment he set foot in the door, the relevant papers were signed and I awaited the arrival of the Cheque, it came through a week or so later, I paid it immediately into my current account and drew the money out as soon as it cleared, there was enough for my bird and some nice treats for the family, so everyone was happy, we each had one of these policies and it was my choice to cash it in early so please don't think I was being selfish or depriving my family before my own needs, we always paid the bills first and whatever money was over went into a holiday fund so we could have a week at the seaside once a year.

So off I headed to Newent a big bulge of cash in my pocket and a chilli con carne I had made to take down, I think at one point me and Simon got quite competitive about it but in a good way, as I remember I arrived in the evening we ate the chili and the usual banter ensued mines better than yours etc a few beers then to sleep, the next day Simon took me down and showed me my male Harris he was out on a bow perch on the middle lawn, he's a belter I said, Simon agreed and said he was a good bird, I met up with Mima in the old weighing room which used to be next to the little museum and entrance and thanked and paid for my new little charge, Simon helped me put fresh equipment on him he was placed in a cardboard box with air holes and off cut of carpet in the bottom for him to grip onto, I had intention of breaking the sound barrier on the way home but it was there to make him feel more secure for the drive home you cannot predict if someone is going to pull out on you or cut you up it's all about thinking ahead I guess, anyway my theory of driving is, if you assume everyone driving on the roads is an idiot and don't know what they are doing you won't go far wrong!, woodbine was loaded up into the back of the fiesta and off I set back home, The journey is pretty much all motorway and takes me around 1 1/2 hours taking it steady, which is less time to keep a bird in a box, I arrived home that afternoon allowing plenty of time before it got dark so I could settle him into his new quarters, as I previously mentioned I had a flight some 18 feet long, sand on the floor, a short tree stump, bath and a concrete slab to pop food through onto during the moult, oh one end was a fixed perch, and the other end I had made a sort of trapeze swinging perch with some bungee cord, all in all a splendid new home for my new little friend, he had been already trained which didn't worry me as he had been "Falconry Centre" trained so I knew it had been done properly, I popped him in the flight filled the bath up with fresh water stayed in there a while with him then left him too it for the night.

"Woodbine" at weighing time

I had found some new Flying ground, George, my wife Paula's uncle had a friend who was a market gardener and had expressed his disdain at all the rabbits that were eating his "bleedin" produce, when George told him I had a hawk he near fell over himself to invite me to come fly anytime I wanted, and it was only a mile or two up the road, perfect, I had taken the week off work so we could get used to each other, the next day we loaded up and headed off to inspect our new flying ground again we had many acres to roam over with a stream at the bottom with trout in and a couple of woods a lot of different places to explore, I got him following along nicely, following ahead and flying from the fist he was happy doing any of the above, I think I had a couple of months flying him before it was time to be put up for the moult, hunting birds are usually put up in the summer so they can grow new feathers, I mean in the wild obviously a wild bird wouldn't stop flying for the moult they just carry on as they need to eat feed young, but with hunting birds it is the usual thing to do, the summer passed slowly and I was really keen to get out there again.

It was by now the beginning of September, so he was caught up, fresh equipment fitted telemetry mount new Jesse's and his beak "coped", coping is akin to ladies filing their finger nails to keep them in good shape, and sometimes birds need a little help with this, again it is totally painless and small files are used to gently take off excess growth, I had been gradually lowering his weight since he finished his moult so it wasn't many days before he responded, and we were back to where we was earlier in the year, I love being out in the countryside this time of year watching the leaves change colour and fall, beautiful, on this one particular outing we were walking up the hill towards a round hilltop wooded area, Woodbine was flying ahead tree to tree as I followed up tapping the hedge, when all of a sudden, he shot out of the tree he had just taken stand in, heading back down the hill and went crashing into some brambles in the wood that bordered the stream at the bottom I tore down after him with the telemetry on and when I finally got there after humping my way carefully through waist high brambles there he sat on quite a big hen pheasant, my initial jubilation and celebrations were soon cut short as I heard an approaching quad bike, oh crumbs, I'm sure this wood isn't on Peter the market gardeners land, the quad bike got closer and I thought oh dear I'm in trouble it was the game keeper he jumped off the quad bike and came marching over to me, and with the language of old country charm he said, "and what the f***K are you doing in here, I'm not the confrontational sort at best and I think he saw that, I replied I'm really sorry, he took off, came crashing into here and I had to follow, pointing to Woodbine on the ground hen pheasant firmly in his grip, "oh" he said a male Harris, what weight you flying him at I felt all the tension leave my body and relief I told him and we stood chatting, turns out he used to look after the hawks and falcons of his employer who was at the time the chairman of the BFC, (The British Falconers Club), we ended up laughing and getting on famously, he said look tell you what, if you stay out of here and wait till the shooting season is done after the last shoot you can come in here and hunt all you want, I thanked him and almost fell over with shock and delight at his kindness, I took out my little diary and penciled in the date when the last shoot was, and true to my word I stayed out of the wood, it was hard to keep Woodbine out, as a couple of times he went back, but managed to call him out before anything was to catch his eye, I would take him to the other end of the land and there we hunted for rabbits, we flew over that land for a few seasons keeping to my word and both of us eating well on pheasants and rabbits.

The only time I ever lost Woodbine was entirely my own fault, I had been taking him out in the afternoons and staying till dusk or just before, on the fateful day in question he was a little high in weight, there is an old saying, "If a hawk is high do not fly", ignore this at your peril, also if the wind is high do not fly well, That is my unwritten rule anyway, common sense should tell us that this is not a wise thing to do, but as we all know common sense sometimes eludes us, on the day in question we went about things the normal way, that day I chose to fly him following on, rather than from the fist, he had caught a hen pheasant and had managed to get a few beak fulls down him the time it took me to get to him, he had caught it the other side of the stream so I had walk back almost back to the car where the small bridge was and walk all the way back up, I didn't fancy jumping over it as it was just a little too far across, I had previously tried the same trick earlier in the year and came unstuck "splosh", so the point being he had quelled his appetite somewhat, with eating some of the pheasant and the tiny peanut sized offerings I gave him occasionally as we walked round, I should have stopped, put on his swivel and leash and gone home, but I didn't, I thought I will just let him follow me back to the car and then we can go home... "wrong" yes he did follow me back to the car and landed in quite a big oak tree close by no amount of gentle coaxing enticing with the pickup piece of meat or indeed some quite colourful swearing would make him budge, "bugger", he drew up one leg and sat there all fluffed out, now I had two choices I could spend the night in the car and try and get him down first light, before he could move, or go home some 2 miles away go to bed and come back before first light, so I waited there till it was pitch black, and he wasn't going to move, and decided to go back home and return before first light, as soon as I got in I telephoned the land owner and made him aware of what was going on, I didn't want him worrying seeing car headlights, and me poking around there before dawn, well I didn't sleep at all, I ended up reading most of the night, looked at the clock and thought sod it, it was an hour before first light so I set off back to the field and parked up I could see with a torch he was still where I had left him, and I was still getting a signal from his transmitter, so I had backup if he did decide he still wasn't hungry enough to come down!, as it got light I was there ready and waiting and I breathed a sigh of relief as he gently glided down to my glove, " you little bugger I said I thought I had lost you", never again was I to risk flying a hawk that was too high in weight, the lesson had been firmly learned, I could almost hear Phillip whispering, "you won't do that again will you"?.

Flying continued as normal a couple of days later and the events of the previous days was soon forgotten, but I can tell you the first time I let him fly up into a tree again my heart was in my mouth even knowing everything was fine again, but that is just me, we used to go right to the other side of the land to stay away from the pheasant wood as I called it, it went slightly uphill but once at the top it was a lovely view over the other side at the top, there was a big round wood that covered the hilltop and it gently sloped away down below to a hedge some 200 yards away downhill so a perfect place to be at the top on one particular afternoon Woodbine was in a tree about fifteen feet above my head, I had sat down at the top and had backed into the thick hedge that surrounded the hilltop wood, I was partially covered, Woodbine was quite happy, then the most amazing thing happened, to my left no more than 12 feet away came a rustling sound from the hedge bottom and out stepped as calm as you like a young vixen fox I sat perfectly still as she stepped out and she quietly sat down, so there we were Woodbine above me in the tree, and me and the fox sitting in the edge of the hedge looking down the hill, it seemed like an eternity but in reality no More than a few minutes, she turned her head looked right at me turned on her heels and disappeared back into the hedge, I was utterly amazed, and I couldn't wait to get back home and tell my family, they said I'm not surprised said Paula my wife, you have a sort of affinity with animals, which I seem to have, everything seems to make a beeline for me especially Labradors when I have a sandwich in my pocket.

Even on the days we couldn't fly I would always bring him inside for an hour or so, we would either put the TV on or listen to the radio, I can honestly say I spent a minimum of an hour a day everyday with him throughout the flying season if bad weather torrential rain or gales stopped us from hunting, I have always made a point of animals and birds get fed before I do even on Christmas day I would feed him before myself and this habit has stayed with me to present day, I personally think it adds another element of appreciation towards our little two or four legged friends.

12 LABRADORS

Labradors, all I can say is they are the "best dog in the world", my first ever contact with these lovely dogs was when I worked at Newent and a black Labrador called Bramble, as I remember she was a law unto herself and would wander around the house and grounds and I might not see her for hours, or you could be in the flying ground and she would appear right in the bottom corner of the field wagging her tail, up to something I'm sure, she really did have a lovely disposition, during the summer months I slept in a caravan that was at the back of the car park and she would often follow me back there and help me eat whatever goodies I had there, Labradors seem to have the habit of being in the right place at the right time when food is around I would often see the visitors trying to eat there picnics with a salivation Labrador sitting close and watching every morsel go from hand to mouth a lot like watching heads move left to right whilst watching a tennis match at Wimbledon, sometimes she would come back in the evenings and curl up on the bottom of my bed, I knew one day I would love to own one of these lovely animals.

We got our first house 1983, in fact we moved into it on New Year's Day 1983, Christmas tree and all, I wouldn't recommend it, it was freezing cold and although not much traffic on the roads it was still a major upheaval, everything we owned which wasn't much was bundled into a big white transit van and a few runs later we were in, just in time for a nice glass of red wine before bed.

I knew this was the right time to set about looking for a Labrador puppy, I started off my asking my vet at the time if he knew of anyone breeding labs in the area, he did, and gave me the telephone number to some kennels, where the owner Mary lived and she breed labs that were field trial champions, so I got on the phone that evening and made arrangements to go and visit on my next day off, Thursday soon came a around and I followed the sketchy directions, turn right at the railway bridge over the river past the hall on the left, turn right as you go up the hill follow the lane to the nasty left hand bend and turn right, good god I managed to find it the first time, the last two lanes were only wide enough for one car so if I had met the village bus coming the other way I would have been well and truly scuppered!, I pulled up at the house with dogs barking from every direction, I caught a glimpse of a few of the labs through the fencing they looked first class, I knocked on the front door almost immediately a small lady with a weathered face and tightly permed hair flung the door open wide stepped past me and shouted, and I mean shouted loudly "SHUT UP"!!, and as if my magic silence fell over the place in almost the same breath she turned to me and said hello, you must be Chris, I'm Mary and reached out her hand to shake mine, what a character Mary was, she was very much old school, slightly eccentric but all the best people are, we were to become good friends, so you want a Labrador do you she said without mincing her words, well I'll need to see where you live and make sure your home and you are suitable I think I giggled nervously, which she returned with a glare, hmm she said come on this way, and I followed along behind through various gates, shut the gate she stated, mind that there, don't trip she came across very coarse but when we finally got to the runs where her labs were and she was amongst them you could see her heart melt, and I got a glimpse of her true nature, salt of the earth what you see is what you get, don't they call that wizzywig or something WYSIWYG? I think so, she showed me her various stud dogs and bitches I was impressed they looked strong and healthy and well cared for, right she said there are no litters at the moment, so you are going to have to wait, OK Mary, I replied she grumbled something about pencil and paper so we headed back to the house, and she took my name address and telephone number, now, when is a good time for me to come and visit?, I said something like well I get Thursdays off work and she muttered something about well at least you have a job that is a bloody bonus, or weekends, we arranged that she would call on Saturday morning at 9:30, and true to her word she arrived bang on 9:30, I opened the door to her and said glibly your right on time come in, "can't stand people that are late, as she stepped in, hello she said as she walked up to my wife your his better half I see?, I felt kind of detached from this inspection I guess it was, you have a lovely big back garden she exclaimed, we do indeed, I know the area well plenty of room for a dog and you have the woods on your doorstep, tea was made and poured, biscuits offered, we all chatted for around an hour

Mary said well I'm happy with you and where you live so we can go ahead then I felt somehow relieved we had passed the test with flying colours, I wish everyone that were thinking of a dog or even a hawk had a "Mary" to vet and inspect them first!, right as I said she continued there are no litters at the moment but I have your telephone number so as soon as there is one I will be in touch.

Around 6 months passed when one day the phone rang, hello its Mary came the voice, now she said there is a litter, but there are three people ahead of you, are you still off on a Thursday she inquired, I am I replied OK I will pick you up, and take you over to see them, oh, thank you I replied, your most welcome, although she came across in a "coarse country" way Mary had impeccable manners and expected everyone else to as well and she had no problem about speaking her mind, a time was arranged and yet again exactly on time the door knocked and there she was, are you ready, got no time to hang about need to get back and feed the dogs we grabbed our coats and off we went.

Mary must have been in her early 70's at the time and drove a little Suzuki 4x4, the three of us climbed in no sooner had we turned out of our road, and onto the lane all of a sudden we came to a screeching halt, "wind your window down she remarked", I did so without hesitation for fear of being hung, excuse me she shouted across me, with me leaning right back and as far down in the seat as I could, that dogs too fat!!, this woman was walking a Labrador and yes it was overweight, you are killing it you know, she said, you need to get it on a diet, I don't remember the woman saying anything in her defense she just stood there shocked, but of course she was right the dog was overweight, "these bloody people" she said have these dogs and don't look after them, come on wind your window up we need to get on, we drove off with her muttering something about, she could do with losing a few pounds too I desperately had to stifle my laughter, or I might get in trouble too, after 40 minutes or so we arrived at a farm with a huge house, a very well dressed and very posh sounding lady came out to greet us, and walked us over to a stable block in a small courtyard, we were beckoned inside by a man all in tweeds and a flat cap, there were a few other people in there too having a look, a sort of big square had been made inside with straw bales and a heater lamp hung down over mother and pups they looked adorable, how are they doing Mary asked the chap in the tweeds and flat cap all good Mary, all good he replied, I gathered from the conversation that Mary had been present at the birth and woe betide any of them that didn't stand to attention after they were born I said to myself in my head, people were asking various questions of the man and lady, when can we have one etc, we were told they would be ready to go in a couple of months, so I penciled in a rough date in my little diary I always carried, one couple there were particularly chatty, the wife seemed OK but I could see Mary glaring at the husband, he was a bit of a comedian and to be honest he never shut up, Paula got chatting to his wife and I thought oh god no I can't be doing with him yapping constantly down my ear, he was a chiropodist by trade which everyone in the stable knew within ten minutes of him being there, maybe he was touting for business, I thought well you can piss off he isn't going anywhere near mine, he remarked I would like that one, Mary replied well if you was first in the queue maybe, but you are not now be quiet, again stifling my laughter he kind of pulled a face as if to say that told me, it was amusing, I asked Mary later and they had approached her as their own black lab had recently died and they were beside themselves, Mary said she is lovely but he's a bit of a nightmare.

During the two months wait we got as much ready as is possible, Mary was a great help and really you don't need that much, we knew what they were being fed etc and it was just a matter of waiting, the time passed slowly when we finally got a phone call to say they were ready, this time we arranged to meet Mary there as she had already travelled over to the farm earlier that day, it had just got dark when we arrived, saw Mary and she beckoned us over to the stable block, OK were all here now the lady said, the man with the flat cap said ready? And then opened the stable door and they all tumbled and scrambled into the yard some people picked them up and the man and Mary carefully watched the puppies and us, the man said OK Mary who is first?, Mary replied that gentleman and pointed to one of the people we had seen before, he looked like a shooting man to me, and the man with the flat cap pointed to him and said OK your choice, he pondered a while and picked up a pup "this one" I think, as it licked his nose we had paid Mary a couple of weeks previously for our pup, everyone made their choice and left, Mary, and the man with the flat cap were constantly watching and counting the pups, as Mary explained it was unknown for someone to pick up a pup in all the confusion and hide it under a big coat or something, anyway I think I was third to choose the man in the flat cap and his wife, who owned the farm had already chosen a pup and she was holding it in her arms, Paula whispered to me, "you choose" so I stepped forward, I had no idea which one, I knew I wanted a bitch, so I stood for a while, Mary said take your time there is no rush, she could see I was getting a little agitated and couldn't make up my mind, I was looking for something some sign of uniqueness and then I saw it, one of the little buggers had climbed up on top of the muck heap in the yard, and it was black, I said to the man in the flat cap "I would like that one please if it's a bitch, he climbed up in his wellies picked it up and said yep it is a bitch and handed it over to me, put her inside my coat with her head peeping out, and "Teal" came to stay, we said our thanks and goodbyes to the nice couple that owned the farm, Mary said she would pop in during the week to see how we were getting along.

Teal settled in pretty quickly, of course we had the inevitable wincing for a few nights but this was soon sorted and calm returned to the Jauncey household at night, whilst I was waiting to pick her up I had found a secondhand kennel made from match board with a 2"x2" framework, it resembled a Large coal shed, painted dark with a tiny entrance in the middle, I would soon change this, I sanded it all down with a borrowed from a friend belt sander, which saved a lot of puffing and wheezing on my part, in the front I cut out a small window, and made a slot in shutter type one with a row of ventilation holes along the top for when we had clad or bad weather, and on the other side of the front I made a small stable door, standing back,", much better I thought, now plenty of fresh air could circulate around inside, a friend who was a welder and used to repair and build new pens for Twycross Zoo had some 3" square galvanized mesh over from a job he had just done, and duly dropped it off in his van, the pieces were big enough for me to add a sort of detachable run onto the front some 8feet deep and 4 feet high.

Teal continued to grow over the following months and with Mary's help I trained her to the whistle, so I had a well behaved biddable Lab, or so I thought!.

I had a phone call at work one day.

It was Paula, this bloody Labrador of yours she said in not a very good mood, what's she done thinking she had urinated on the kitchen tiles, oh no, she had done something far worse, it transpired that she thought there is better food in the fridge and had in the course of opening it chewed off the seal completely from around the door, eaten anything worth having from inside, which turned out to be 1 large family trifle, a whole cooked chicken six eggs shells cracked open and eaten, one packet of butter UN-opened, left the margarine, she obviously had good taste!!, good god, Paula was fuming, I better telephone Mary I thought. it was the whole cooked chicken containing the bones that concerned me, I was really not looking forward to telephoning Mary as I knew she was going hit the roof, but I also knew she would give clear concise advice with no frills attached, hi Mary I have a problem, what's wrong she said, I recounted the story to her the phone fell silent for a moment then roars of laughter, this has to be a good sign I said to myself, OK she said you need to bung her up with brown bread and weetabix to bind her, after what she had just eaten I thought I doubt she will get any of that down, I thanked her then telephoned Paula back, and relayed the message, I later found out when I arrived home she had wolfed all that down too, crisis averted, there was only one other occasion when she did this just after actually, where she got into the cupboard and had flour and gravy powder mashed all into her face, we gave her the run of the house and this behaviour stopped thankfully, but Teal was to remain a thief all her life. One Christmas I remember it quite clearly, I had put the turkey in the oven before bed and cooked it through the night, we used to buy a lovely fresh one from the farm nearby every year, sadly the family sold up and they have built these awful looking houses on there, so in the morning I got up and we had a huge piece of pork to cook as well, I think we had 7 for dinner that year, later that morning a friend of ours who was a nurse was having a few drinks round her house before Christmas dinner as she was working herself on Christmas day, so the oven was switched off

I took out the big piece of pork that was cooked to a turn and placed it on an old willow pattern server type plate that had always been dusted off every year for the Christmas roast, put it on the work surface and pushed it to the back, our nurse friend only lived some 30 yards away so it was a short walk, the house was full of life and people it was really nice, we had a few drinks and headed back home an hour or so later, I walked into the kitchen something was missing, I looked around, "where is the pork I asked, you put it on a plate came the reply I know I did but where have you moved it too I haven't touched it came back the reply the plate was still where I had left it, absolutely squeaky clean, and then I looked at teal she was laying asleep and looked like she had eaten a football!!, yes that is right she had eaten the whole piece of pork, completely, and even managed to get it off the side without breaking the plate, that Christmas dinner was a little light but couldn't help seeing the funny side, animals really do brighten up our days even if we do not see it at the time.

From time to time Mary would pop down and see how we were getting along, she became a family friend and we was always glad to see her, she invited me out to a field trial on one occasion which was great fun, and very interesting to watch the dogs work, it was on one of these events she said to me, you know Teal would be good to have a litter of pups off, I replied along the lines of do you really think so? Yes came the reply, so on returning home I had a chat with Paula and we decided to go ahead, we were to keep one, and Mary assured me that the others would be found good homes for, shooting homes too, the little kennel and run I had built would become invaluable, it was used to pop Teal in when we went shopping or out, sometimes whether summer or winter I would look around for her at bedtime to find her laying down in the kennel on the bed quite happy, she was as happy outdoors as in, a day was arranged to take teal up to Marys and get mated, which I had to do three times in all before she would have anything to do with another dog, in the way of being mated, then it was just a waiting game as she got bigger and bigger, I drove over to Lichfield to Staffordshire farmers and bought one of those infrared heater lamps with a big aluminium shade on and set about wiring it up over the bed inside the kennel to keep the pups warm, in fact when turned on it got quite cozy in there, as Teals time grew closer Mary made frequent visits to check on me, I felt like a nervous first time father!.

It was time, I can remember Teal waddling out and laying down in the wooden plywood bed I had made, she was panting and not far off, there was enough room inside for me to sit quite comfortably next to the bed, I had even fitted a small bolt to the inside of the stable door so I could close it too from the inside and keep draughts out, she had shown signs at around 7:00pm in the evening and I could see this wasn't going to happen fast, the kennel and run was just outside the kitchen door on a medium sized concrete yard, so it was quite handy for nipping in and out as the night dragged on, I think she started at around 9:00pm and out popped one after the other, 5 little black Labrador puppies, nature is amazing, I had never before witnessed the birth of puppies, Teal was so calm and I couldn't quite believe she had allowed me so close, in fact so close one was actually born on my lap, she was having trouble breaking open the membrane that surrounds them so I helped, and as she licked it and I gently rubbed the little puppy it took a breath, I knew that this one was going to be special and I was going to keep this one, it was always the plan to keep this one, I kept an eye on her as she grew and painted one of her claws carefully with Paula's red nail varnish so I didn't mix them up, when your close with a litter like this and see them everyday, you get to know each puppy and tell by the slightest difference which is which but always to be sure I kept up with the nail polish, I thought it was all over and I went inside for a mug of tea and promptly fell asleep on the sofa, I startled myself awake it was 5:30, I gathered myself up and went to see the pups, "who's put two yellow pups in here was my first reaction!, as while I had slept she had given birth to another two puppies both yellow, they were just as gorgeous, Teals mother had been yellow, but for some reason I was expecting all black, Mary popped along later that morning and gave Teal and the puppies once over, she was as good as a vet, and everything was fine, and now the hard work began, they grew rapidly and looking after puppies became my full time job, I was no longer working for the high street electrical retailer so my days were all my own.

From 6:00am till around 10:00pm my day was taken up looking after the pups, it was an endless cycle of feeding and then clearing up after them, once they had all done there business and all cleaned up I would love to get in the kennel with them they would scramble all over me licking or nibbling my ears they were great fun and I didn't want any of them to go, anyone that breeds dogs for money need their heads looking at, and although they were going to be sold to their new owners the money would not cover the costs involved, and for me it was never about the money, Mary would telephone or when she visited asked if so and so could come up and see the pups, and a gradual stream of people from the shooting world came along chatted and saw the pups, and it was not long before they were ready to go, as the various people came and took them my heart sank a little, but was counter balanced by the thought that they all were headed for good homes and for me it was better they went one at a time, the last one had gone and I was left with the little black one and has anyone guessed yet what I was going to name her?, no?, well it was "Bramble", I knew from the moment she popped out on my lap that is what I was going to name her.

Bramble was totally opposite to her mum, she didn't steal and had the most wonderful gentle disposition of any Lab I have ever seen, and she would happily walk by my side on or off the lead, I had many happy years with them both, walking them around the local wood and watching them snuffle around in the fallen leaves in Autumn I miss them both very much even to this day I have one last memory to add and hope you will forgive me, when it finally came Brambles time to leave me it was summer she was quite an old girl and would prefer to sleep out in the garden as she got progressively less able to walk about it was a particularly warm summer so I bought one of those gazebos to put over her and a bed for her to lay in, I would sit out there with her for hours on end and we would watch the bees busy about their work or maybe a mouse looking for a meal, Bramble finally went off her legs completely and stopped drinking her water, so I reluctantly telephoned the vets, about an hour Later a young Vet arrived with even a nurse, he examined her and said to me, "you already know what I am going to say to you don't you?, I nodded without saying a word, he carefully shaved a little hair off the side of her paw, I said "wait", I pulled her completely onto my lap, I said OK you can continue now, I forced out the words, She was born on my lap and she will go out the same way, and my dear little bramble slipped peacefully away, and I sat there on my own sobbing like a baby for a good half hour, another chapter in my life had ended.

13 BLACK CATS & HENS

It was many years after I lost my beloved Labradors Teal &
Bramble that I could face taking on another four legged friend, it had
upset me that deeply, I can remember a particular day in early
summer I had been in the garden tending to my vegetable plot, and I
had come indoors to make a nice hot mug of tea, I had left open the
back door as usual much to the annoyance of my wife who always
shouting, "shut that door", when I happened to glance up the garden,
there standing looking back down at me was the prettiest Black Cat I
have ever seen it sort of caught my gaze, to emphasize the point on
how unusual this was, cats had never ever come in my garden before,
maybe because we had always had Labradors and were doggie people,
a term which to be honest I dislike, your either "animal" people or
you are not, and anything with four legs to me was equal, why dog
and cat people hate each other I have no clue really, anyway I stood
looking at this black cat, and before I could even think, something
inside me prompted me to say to it, "well you better come in then
and get something to eat", and to my utter amazement it bloody well
did to, and sat at my feet looking up at me, hmm I thought, "ah yes
sardines" I said part talking to myself part to the cat and into the
cupboard I went digging away, and found a can of sardines, emptying
them onto a saucer I placed it down in front of the black cat, to
which it tucked right in scoffing the lot, it then walked into the
lounge as if it owned the place and fell asleep on the stairs, I was
utterly amazed, I had gone from Black Labradors to Black cats, it was
as if some all great animal spirit above and saw how lonely I was and
sent me this beautiful black cat to look after.

The cat continued to visit me for a week, my daughter, who
calls in from work everyday at lunchtime to see me was also shocked
but pleased for me, we chatted and decided that I should make
efforts to locate the owner, as it did have a collar and well, it was the
right thing to do, Paula made inquiries around the neighbourhood
and a woman a few streets away was identified as the cats owner I
was a little upset but I was not the owner, Paula went around
knocked on the door, she answered and I said, "I think your cat has
been visiting me", she said "I have had two new kittens, and have not

seen him for days", she walked back round with me calling him and he reluctantly followed her back down the path, I even offered to take him on if she felt overloaded with cats, to me it was pretty obvious by the way she spoke that he had his nose pushed out, anyway I was left once again without a daytime companion, my daughter Kate said "I'll get you a cat dad", which was a lovely thought, and I agreed.

I had always loved black cats, I had a memory from an early age of my mum giving to me a little black cat made in glass, that she had been given to by her piano teacher for passing an exam, over the years during moving it had gotten lost, but no matter as I can remember it to this very day, and as long as I can remember that little glass figure, to me it is as good as having it to hold, I can never remember her playing the piano as we never owed one, they were expensive items in the late fifties early sixties, but my dad many years after recounted to me that listening to her playing the Warsaw concerto moved him to tears every time, written in 1941 by Richard Addinsell for the film Dangerous Moonlight, about the Polish struggle against the Nazi invasion of Poland in 1939, and I have to say it has the same effect on me these days as well, it is a short piece under ten minutes long but is very beautiful and emotive, as it brings her to mind immediately, I can be honest in saying that I still miss her everyday, and I hang onto the few childhood memories I have left, with determined and passion.

I started to look on cat rescue sites in the area, and there looking back at me was another black cat, not too far away from me, I showed Paula and Kate, and I telephoned the group and a day was arranged for me to go over and have a look, it was about a 40 minute drive, and we more or less went right to the house, I parked up and we rang the doorbell, a young woman answered, "oh you must be Chris?", nodding she let me in, well there were bloody cats everywhere, we were shown into the lounge "sit here, and I will go get her, but I have to warn you she said, she has bitten and clawed everyone that has come to see her with a view to adopting, I will take my chance I quipped smiling, and she popped upstairs to fetch "Ebony", she appeared a few moments later, plonking this black cat on my lap, which proceeded to lick my hand and fall asleep, "well she said" I can't believe it, she has bitten everyone, I just smiled and thought, the old Chris animal charm must be at 100% again, we chatted for a while, and the young woman said someone will be in touch, and we left, heading back home.

A few days later Paula took a phone call from the head cheese at the Cat Rescue Centre, and a day was arranged for her to vet us, this should be fun I thought, anyway she duly arrived at our door at the pre- arranged time, things were already off to a good start as she was punctual, I admire that quality in people, and in she stepped carrying a large cat carrier, sitting herself on the sofa she remarked, "Well I have already had a look around the area and it is perfect for a cat, no main roads, with a huge expanse of green to the rear, and now meeting you she said after a few minutes, were quite happy for you to take on the little black cat, do you have any questions, pulling my mouth to one side and kind of struggling to ask something just to appear on the same page, I mean how hard is it to look after a cat?, I appreciated her professionalism, god knows what sort of people she met in role as "cat vetter", and I asked, "erm, where do they sleep?", "anywhere they want", the reply came right back, which caused us all to chuckle which broke the ice.

The door to the carrier was quietly open and we all sat there bated breath, after a few moments the little black cat carefully placed a paw out on the carpet, slowly and surely moving out and into the room, she is beautiful I whispered, look how long her tail is the women from the cat group softly remarked, and with that the little black cat shot around the back of the sofa and barely came out for a couple of days, that is normal the woman remarked, with that we signed the adoption paper and she left bidding us good luck and goodbye, and "Ebony" came to stay.

As I was pretty much house bound, I had all day to talk to Ebony, I would offer her tit bits to encourage her out, she was very shy indeed, what we did know about her was that she had been rescued from a drug dealers home, where she had been abused, and more importantly had been rescued by a man, who took her home for a few weeks, but because of his work commitments could not keep her, and I think this had a lot to do with the way she behaved for me, she felt safe with a man, and if a female went near her she would swipe out with a paw, scratching them, sometimes to my quiet amusement, especially if one came that said, "oh I have had hundreds of cats they just need love", reaching out a hand to stroke then withdrawing it with an "ooo you little bastard etc", hilarious.

I was sitting transfixed to the TV one morning, in the house on my own, when I saw something black out the corner of my eye sneaking around my feet, softly and without making a sound, the little black cat jumped up onto my lap, curled up and went to sleep, allowing me to stroke her, I must have sat there for a few hours not daring hardly to move, but I was busting for a wee, so I carefully slid her off my lap onto a blanket next to me, and from that moment on she happily explored her new home, she slept for many years under my arm each night and seemed to feel safe with me, and I can honestly say she has never caused any damage in and around the home to this day, fingers crossed.

Some years passed, and guess what?, another black kitten came into our lives, another unwanted animal, she was as black as Ebony, but much more naughty, thinking nothing of running up the curtains etc, "Izzy" as my son named her came to stay, so we had gone from having two black Labradors to two black cats, and I love them both dearly, I'm sure that there is room for another Black Labrador but I think I would be in very hot water indeed if I announced the desire to have another, we will see.

A few years previously we had a pair of call ducks wandering freely in the garden, "Harold and Henrietta, I put in a large pond for them, and made them a smart little house that we would put them to bed in, they were adorable and I wondered then about having a few hens for eggs, one fateful night we forgot, well I did, to shut the door on the pen with the ducks in, and a fox came into the garden and took them both, I was beside myself, it slipped my mind, and they paid the price, if it had been another night who knows if the outcome would have been different, we shall never know, so the idea on having hens was shelved for almost 20 years.

A neighbour of mine and offered me an 8x6 shed that he no longer wanted, my existing 6x6 shed that I had previously used for a weighing, come equipment room for my hawks was about falling down, so I set about tearing it down an replacing it with the kindly donated newer shed, I had slightly altered the site and this left an empty 12x6 plot, "Hens" I thought, I'm going to get some laying hens, and with that I headed off to the computer to "Google" hen breeders in my location.

The breeders or anything in fact that is "close by", does not make them the best, and I found a breeder of good laying hens about 40 to 50 minutes away, so I headed off with Tom in the car, as soon as we arrived you could tell they really cared for the hens as all the enclosures etc were in pristine condition and kept clean, we picked "Gold Star Rangers" as they were placid and laid a fair few eggs a year, and were a lovely brown colour, we bought 4, a sack of mixed corn, sack of layers pellets and the drinker and feeder, as it was all very reasonably priced, the hens were put into a large cardboard box, and we headed off home.

I had knocked up an enclosure with some old 2x2 timber some 10x6 feet with a door and a wooden hen house was purchased from an online auction site, and it fitted snugly inside, we placed the cardboard box into the run and they all piled out and were soon at home in there lovely new surroundings.

They all settled in a lot quicker than I expected, in fact a couple of hours after they arrived we had our first egg, remarkable really, over the next few weeks we started to get an egg from each, so we were getting four eggs a day, nothing quite tastes like a fresh egg for your breakfast, the ones we did not eat were given away to family and close neighbours.

Although over time we have lost a few from natural causes we still have hens to this day, I do not think the place would be quite the same without them, they are a part of the garden scene.

14 BLACK DOG, PABLO-PIPPIN

This is probably one of the hardest chapters for me to write, I have debated long and hard whether or not to write about the awful illness that has blighted my life, as I do not want to come across as "woe is me", but equally I think to totally ignore this dark part of my life would be wrong as would not get to understand things from my perspective, the one resounding thought in my head which convinced me to write a small section on this was, if one person, just one reads this, and it helps them realize they are not alone, they can live with depression, and it saves one life, then laying myself bare will be well worthwhile.

For me it started in 1992 when I awoke standing on the wall of a river bridge, and an old lady tugging at my trouser leg saying, "what are you doing", "are you OK?", without my knowledge, I had woken that morning, washed, put on my business suit and driven to work, to this day I cannot remember doing this, my day started with me standing on that river bridge staring down at the cold fast flowing water with that little old lady tugging and talking me back into reality, I never found out who she was but she undoubtedly saved my life, there are no words or actions that can possibly express how grateful I was to her, for that one act of kindness, for her just caring enough to stop and see if she could help me, I hope one day I am able to help someone else this way.

Back then people were scared of the words "mental illness", we had a lot of friends couples who we used to go out for meals with the pub etc, and I can remember one particular couple that stand out and shall remain nameless, the woman was a childhood friend of my wife's and we had been friends for years, Paula my wife had persuaded me to leave the house and were going to pop round just for a cup of tea and a chat, it was all arranged and we arrived at their home, were greeted and sat in the lounge what followed was probably the most singularly hurtful thing I had ever experienced in my life, she turned to my wife and said,

"Would he like a cup of tea?"

I was sitting right there and yet she addressed the comment to my wife, I was already in a very fragile state of mind and that upset me beyond words, with tears streaming down my face I said I wanted to go home, we left without having the tea, and we never saw them again, at the time I blamed myself, but when I look back now it was "shame on them", no wonder people have a stigma about mental health, which I am pleased to say in the last few years people have put up their hands both ordinary and celebrity and said "you know what, I suffer from that too", on the one occasion I visited a top psychiatrist he told me, "Chris", "only intelligent people suffer from depression", this has always stayed with me, no I'm no better than anyone else, but I am as good as anyone else.

From 1992 until present day I have daily fought against these periods of blackness, Winston Churchill called it, his "Black Dog", so I decided to call my depression my "Black Dog" too, for one I like black dogs, and cats as it happens but most importantly it made me think of black Labradors and that is a positive thought to carry around while fighting off demons.

In the early days I barely left the house except for doctor's appointments, I had pretty much lost interest in life and everything else, then something amazing happened, the Internet arrived, I was given an old computer and we got setup with dial up Internet it was so funny dialling up to connect in those days, and from my home I could visit the world without traveling.

Somewhere around 2007 ish I accepted depression, I can remember saying to myself, OK I have it, I can't do anything about it, so I am going to have to live with it, and get on with my life as best as I can, it did not make the black periods any easier but I knew I would come out OK at the other end sometime or other, so for anyone reading that knows exactly what I am talking about for me accepting that I had it, and was going to have it for the rest of my life somehow liberated me.

2013 rolled in my daughter Kate and her fiance Robert announced that they were going to get married, we were over the moon for them both, they were well suited and we all got on well, after the initial excitement had died down I was hit by a sudden stark thought, I would have to walk my daughter down the aisle, and make a speech in front of maybe a hundred to a hundred and fifty people, I felt the colour drain from my face, I had never been exposed to this many people and had to speak since my days working in Newent, "shit", but I had to do it, somehow it had to be done, it was my place, and I wanted to enjoy it so very much, I had to find a way to kennel the "Black Dog" for one day.

I spent most of the rest of the year worrying about it, stressing because I wanted to be there for my Daughter and not let them down, I never wrote a word of my speech till a few weeks before, I was actually in my little greenhouse planting some seeds, and words began to flow through my head, so I quickly went and sat at my old computer and wrote them down head to mouth, as fast as I could type with two fingers, it looked good and said everything I wanted to, and I read out those very words on the day with very minor alterations.

Finally the morning of the wedding day arrived, and the house was bustling with people, I had showered and dressed well in advance, as I knew once all the girls arrived I would not get a look in for hours, I went off on my own a couple of times and shed some tears, I could already feel my throat going dry and becoming detached from the situation due to fear, "get a grip", I firmly told myself, the car arrived and Kate and I climbed inside, she looked lovely and I felt so very proud of her, in fact I feel very proud of both my children they have never given us any cause for concern, they are both good kids.

We pulled up in the car at the small hotel in Lichfield some seven or eight miles away, and of course we had to pose for photographs, then we walked into the hotel lobby and up the stairs to an anteroom where they do a few formalities, to make sure you are not already married and such, this only took a few minutes, I was sweating and shaking badly, my instincts were telling me to run but I was telling myself to keep calm, we stood outside the doors, they opened, the room was full, and I walked her slowly down the aisle, in fact Kate will not mind me saying I had to slow her pace down a little, for fear of arriving at the front too fast, once I was beckoned to sit down I felt a huge weight lift from me, I turned and smiled at my wife she squeezed my hand, I had done it, and sat back to enjoy the rest of the ceremony.

"This Way", the photographer called us waving a hand above his head and we headed out to the park nearby to take the pictures, the sun had come out so it was quite nice, after all the usual shots were taken we headed back up to the hotel for the "wedding breakfast", it was the middle of the afternoon so not really breakfast but still, the meal was lovely, and now the worst part was approaching my speech, I didn't really eat much as a felt sick, in comes the master of ceremonies, we had agreed prior to the day that Rob would do his speech first, and I would follow him, taking out the piece of paper from my jacket, I fumbled and dropped it, I was shaking, sweating dry throat again, the MC announced, "The father of the bride", and I stood up god knows how, but I did, and carefully began to read from the paper, I could feel the sweat on my brow, but I did it, I bloody well did it, I had managed to do what I never ever thought possible, I did it for love, and had got through the day and let no one down, even managing to dance on the evening a few times, which anyone who knows me well will tell you I never ever do, all in all it had been a wonderful day.

Then social media came along and a particular one where people talk and share images, chat and make contact with old friends and new ones, one chap had put up a picture of his goshawk I think I complimented him on what a lovely bird it was, we got talking and more or less I realized I missed flying and hunting with my birds.

I wrote an email to Mima asking her to be put onto a waiting list for a young male Harris hawk, the next day came the reply back, that yes it was possible, this was around November time, so it would give me almost a year to gather the money together, organize timber, build a suitable pen and replace the essential equipment I would need once again, I think I actually drove Mima crackers with my questions, a lot of it due I now know to lack of confidence, I knew the answers well most of them, then in the following month panic was to follow, Mima announced to me that there was a male Harris hawk at the Centre and it was mine if I wanted it!!, I was speechless and quite overcome by her kind offer, but I had got nothing done, no pen no timber, oh lord I thought, "come on Chris", I thought to myself get your arse in gear and I did, I wrote back saying that I would need some weeks to get a pen up and all was arranged to collect the little chap the end of February, great stuff I thought.

If anyone has had to build a pen through the winter will know it can be pretty tough going, digging out footings in either mud frost or rain or the combination of the three can be quite tiring but also great fun.

The pen slowly took shape, I managed to buy quite a decent little freezer for a good price to store his grub in, I basically bought a huge shed, partitioning the door end off, creating a sort of second door into the pen to stop him escaping when the main door was opened, this little room was to become the equipment room, I still had my old balance type scales and weights, I made two opposing counter tops which I got an off-cut from a kitchen fitter for £5 there was enough to do both sides and it looked very smart indeed, I had a 4x2 piece of ply which I bought a tin of blackboard paint, yes blackboard paint, it is usually on the shelf next to the Tartan paint, and I made a blackboard to record times weight food eaten etc exactly as I had been taught many years Earlier by Phillip, on the inside of the door I had saved a set of coat hooks on a piece of wood this was screwed onto the inside of the main door to hang up gloves leashes etc.

Gone were the old days of carrying your hawk out on the fist to the car which always seemed to draw the wrong kind of attention, everyone now used these black plastic carry boxes, they were reasonably priced, lightweight and you could jet wash them clean, and even better I found a nearly new one on an on-line auction site two thirds cheaper than a new one, I found a supplier of frozen food and once the electrics had been put in by a qualified electrician of course, I ordered and stocked it up ready.

The actual pen part itself was going have the floor covered in pea gravel, there would be a swinging perch, rather like a trapeze used in circus acts, a small shelf perch about 5ft off the ground with a heater tube sitting underneath it providing warmth in really cold periods, oh, and of course a large fiberglass bath which I had saved, and miraculously had escaped damage behind the shed.

To my relief and delight Martin Jones was still selling his falconry equipment so I placed an order for the items I would need,

1x medium length Leash,
1x "D" shaped swivel,
1x medium sized Aylmeri eyelet kit,
1x pair of Aylmeri bracelets (anklets) and mews Jesse's,
1x pair of permanent fixed field Jesse's.

I still had my hawking bag, glove and a selection of bells especially made for hawks which I had bought some twenty odd years earlier and were in pretty good shape as I had not had much wear out of them they would be fine, yes I had made the deadline somehow the pen was finished, the freezer was stocked out with a good selection of food for him.

Finally the day arrived to collect my new little charge, sandwiches were made, carry box and all the equipment to fit him out was taken along, and I set off with my lad Tom early one Saturday morning at the end of February.

We arrived early before opening time, and had a drink before going in, finally the museum door opened, I explained to the woman who seemed to be in charge, that I had an appointment with Mima, she got on a walkie talkie thing, and a moment or two later she entered the museum surround as always by her beloved Labradors, she very graciously let me hug her, it had been over 24 years since my last visit and it might as well of been yesterday, I felt right at home, we were taken to a side room where we deposited the carry box and equipment, and was introduced to Holly the curator of birds, we smiled and shook hands, Mima then showed us the smart new hospital building with freshly installed quarters for the sick birds, each compartment had a sliding draw for ease of cleaning and placing food without having to open the doors causing far less stress to injured, and even possibly injured wild birds, after a good look around, Tom and I had a look around at some of the new barns that had been built, the whole place is wonderfully kept, pens flower beds etc were in tip top condition, my favourite part has to be the white hornbeam avenue that you now pass through into the spacious flying ground, we sat and watched the flying display which as always was amazing, I never tire of watching birds fly, for me there is something magnetic and timeless very difficult to put into words.

"Have you seen the new weighing room Chris?", Mima asked me I shook my head and we stepped into the new building which is now much closer to the flying area, before it used to be at the side of the museum, where the new hospital now takes pride of place, it was much bigger, has hot and cold running water and a huge fridge, I was quite curious to see the large blackboard behind with some of the bird weights in grams, I have always been stubborn to switching to metric, I still use pounds and ounces and feet and inches, and it is a shame we still don't have 240 pennies in a pound, Mima told me that "the kids" mostly used grams nowadays, she disappeared out of the door reappearing shortly after, "Here Tom" she offered Tom a short cuffed glove and plonked the sweetest little Merlin on his gloved hand securing the leash, his face lit up, mine too as I had never held a merlin before in my life, a photo was taken and this lovely memory recorded.

"Tom with a Merlin"

"We better go and get this bird for you then", so gathering up a huge soft net, from the weighing room, we set off to one of the larger barns, we had a quick look through the peephole there were two males in there, both were to be caught up and I was to choose which one I wanted, the four of us quietly entered the huge enclosure, they were perched quite high up, and before you could say "Jack Robinson, Holly was climbing up the heavy gauge mesh wall, and was some 15feet above us, it was like watching spider man, or spider woman in this case, I was very impressed, both birds were caught up, and I chose the one making the most noise Mima quipped, "Well I would have gone for the quiet one myself", and on second thoughts I went for the quiet one, a note was made of the ring numbers and the other male was moved into another enclosure making room I surmised for something else, Harris hawk safely under Mima's arm we headed off up to the hospital where we had left the carry box and equipment, my hands were shaking terribly and I made a fumbled attempt to fit the Jesse's, thankfully Holly stepped in to help and the new equipment was fitted, it had been so long since I had done this I was so grateful for the help this first time, his beak and talons was trimmed nicely, and he popped into the box without much trouble sitting on the perch that spanned across its width inside.

Not wanting to keep him in the box too long Tom and I said ours Goodbyes thanked everyone and headed off home, the weather was still very cool and the journey was around 90 minutes so no chance of him over heating in the travel box.

We arrived safely home, I put the carry box on the worktop in the little weighing room I had constructed, remarkably he stepped straight out onto my glove, he had been trained before Mima had told me so this would probably explain things, I slowly backed up and sat him on the scales, 1lb 12 1/2oz, he was indeed well fed, I recorded his weight on the blackboard fixed to the inside of the inner pen door, and popped him onto the bow perch I had set out for him earlier that morning, and filled up his bath with fresh water, I can remember sitting down on the door step into the pen, I have to be honest I shed a few tears and thought and felt positive about the future, once again I had in my care one of my beloved hawks, he would need my care now everyday of his life, and I was determined to succeed.

"Pablo" as he became known, or of late I call him "Pippin" maybe because he turned out to be a real "pip" and has a great character about him, in the first place.

Several months before Tom had been on a social media site, and had asked a local family who had a dairy farm less than a mile from our home if I could fly a hawk over there land, they very kindly agreed, and this was the deciding factor in taking on as without land to fly there was no point in even contemplating a hawk again.

The very next day I started off his training, well I guess it was more a refresher for him as he had been previously trained, and also a good refresher for me too, it all soon came back to me, I would bring him indoors while I sat at my desk typing with one hand, in fact I spent and still do much of my day with, or around him, we quickly progressed from jumping to the glove for a treat to flying half a field on a creance, a long safety line, I took Pablo up to the farm and we were greeted by the farmer's wife, we introduced ourselves, and was shown all the fields we could go in, it was a dairy farm at the time, sadly not to be for much longer as costs 35p a litre to produce and they were paid 22p a litre for it, madness in anyone's eyes.

One large field there is bordered by a small stream and quite a big wood, perfect I thought for training him to follow on and follow ahead, all this means to non-falconry people is that your bird flies from tree to tree as you walk along, either keeping up with you or following a tree or so ahead, everything was slowly coming back to me, and after several more trips to the farm it was like I had never been away from flying, I felt very fortunate indeed to be able to once again enjoy the countryside with a little hawk as a companion.

It was getting late in the season by now, I walked up the garden, as I do every morning, and there laying on the floor beneath his perch was his deck feather, complete with telemetry transmitter clip, this of course heralded the end of flying, and so began his moult, I continued to visit him every morning to check on him, replenishing his bath water daily, and keeping the inside of the pen as spick and span as is possible, the roof of the pen itself was covered with the long side open, so he could choose to sit in the sun, or even rain if it blew in or right at the back away from inclement weather.

As summer progressed I collected his feathers as they dropped, sticking the tail feathers in a small up turned cardboard box, as I have always done, arranging them in a fan in the same positions as they are on the tail, this also gives me an indication of how far along my birds moult is, never ceases to fascinate me the beauty of a full set of tail feathers looks.

The beginning of September soon came around, and my daily checks had revealed that indeed he had finished dropping and growing his new feathers, and I have to say he looked amazing in his new set of feathers, he looked brand new, and I couldn't wait to get him out flying again.

Over the summer I had gathered up all the new equipment to put on him and arranged it all on the dining table, I roped in Paula to help me as two hands are always better than one, new leather anklets were fitted, a new tail mount for the telemetry was carefully slipped over one of the deck feather quills and nipped gently closed, and his beak trimmed of a little over growth, a bit like a manicure, the mews Jesse's were slipped through the anklets, swivel threaded through leash, and I took him up onto my glove, wow he really did look splendid, he stared at me and gave a loud "Qwaaaaaa", showing his disdain and in dignity of being handled, "how dare you", I guessed he was saying to me, "come along" I softly whispered to him, "you are not dead yet", I quipped, I popped him out on the lawn with a bath, and sat down and had a well-deserved coffee break, "were all set", I pondered as I sat sipping my coffee, cupping my hands around the mug.

"Pablo out on a bow perch"

Once again I began his refresher course, and within no time at all we were back to doing what we both loved, out in the countryside in the fresh air with no one around, absolute bliss, it is like the world melts away and there is nothing but calm, I am sure that everyone who enjoys the countryside feels the same way, of course my "Black Dog" was still a frequent visitor, but however bad things got, I always found the strength to go and check on Pip in his pen every morning, because he was solely dependant on me, he was now loose in his pen so was able to fly around, which made me feel slightly happier, and as soon as my black dog went back to kennels I was out there in the fields with him once again, feeling very fortunate and privileged indeed, just an observation but I hear people talking as I have always been a "people watcher", saying how they want this new car or that new laptop, constantly striving for material gain, for me, and this is my personnel opinion, to be able to open our eyes every morning and be granted a brand new day is the greatest gift we can have, after all once were awake the rest of the day is a bonus, whatever comes our way whether it be good or bad, the next day we are given the chance again to do it all better.

Pablo also had a new trick up his sleeve, I would let go of his field Jesse's and he would fly off, but instead of taking stand in a tree he would fly in a huge circle around me landing back on my glove and seemed to me to be saying, "well come on, where's me tit bit", it was amusing to see, he simply loved to fly, and for me was delightful to see, and be a part of.

As the year grew older and the leaves began to fall from the trees, the fields seemed once again quiet and still, I love the autumn it has always been my favourite time of year, summer is just an inconvenience to be tolerated, it was time for gloves and a hat to keep warm, now, I have one of those heads that whatever hat I have tried to wear to keep warm I look a complete Pratt in, don't ask me why, but I do not have a "Hat Head", so once again I turned to an on line auction site and found a brand new never worn tweed flat cap made by a very well-known country manufacturer, and it was at a fraction of the cost of a new one, as money was always tight I had no problem in buying this way, a few days later the parcel arrived at my door carried by an old school friend, who works for the post office, I shook his hand was really pleased to see him again after many years, we had a brief chat, the usual stuff running down the government and the price of gas and electric, before he headed off again, I shut the door and returned my attention to the parcel opening it carefully, it was indeed the tweed flat cap I had ordered, and it was brand new, I was pleasantly surprised and happy, I popped it on my head, walked into the kitchen where Paula was tidying around, I strutted in hands on hips, "what do you think then" I said, she turned round and said,

"You look like a Pratt", and without cracking her face turned back to carrying on with her tidying up, I near wet myself laughing as this had always been a joke between us, me and my "Hat head", well after all I was going to be in the middle of a field where no one would see me anyway, oh and I do have to say, laughter is better medicine for depression than any pills, if you can laugh everyday at something even if it is yourself, it will grow inside you, and the smile will last.

So the very next day we set out to the farm again, the routine was very much the same, I would go into pips pen with a tit bit on my glove, he would fly to me and eat it, I would fit his mews Jesse's and swivel and leash and pop him on my balance type scales, I weighed him the same way each day, with the same equipment attached as to get an accurate reading, once I had fiddled with the weights adding them and taking them away, he would step up onto my glove, and I would record his weight on the blackboard, then open up the door on his carry box where of his own accord he would pop in, he was as keen to go flying as me, shutting the carry box door and letting the leash slip into the groove on the bottom allowing it to feed under the door and up and around the handle, we then headed through the house and the kitchen picking up the pouch containing his meat that I had prepared beforehand, so with meat pouch and glove on top of the carry box I would pick up the telemetry receiver from the dining table, new cap safely in pocket we would head out to the car, and off to the farm, first job on arrival at farm fit cap on silly head, open tailgate, wellies on, put on hawking bag with meat pouch clipped inside, take out transmitter make sure the battery cap is tight, switch it on, turn on receiver check battery state and signal, turn off receiver, put on glove with a small tit bit, hold end of leash, open carry box door, pip jumps up to my glove and has his tit bit, transmitter is slipped into the tail mount on his tail feather and were pretty much ready to go, I also like to fly him "off the fist", so we would walk around a bit sneaking around gates and hedges, on one particular outing Pip did something really funny, we had been out for a few hours and dusk wasn't far off so we headed back towards the car me on this occasion letting him fly on ahead, we got within 15 yards or so from the car, when he flew onto my head, picked up my cap, carried it and landed on the roof of the car, as if to say, "come on, we've been out for hours, I'm cold and it is getting dark and I

want my dinner", hilarious, and as always no one around to witness this amusing event.

In one of the fields where we fly stands a large oak tree, at its base is a curious bulge, on many an evening I sit here and look over the land, just enjoying the moment, sometimes catching sight of a Hare in the distance, or watching one of the common buzzards that nests in the wood nearby soaring high on a thermal, or a field mouse scratching around in the leaf litter, nature is truly wondrous, often I sit here for an hour or so before heading home, so getting back to how I started off this chapter, anyone can do anything they want to, you just have to believe you can, and yes you can get better and you can live with this very debilitating illness, we will never be the same people we were before, but maybe we find a different kind of strength, but whatever you do never give up, remember, it is OK to get despondent and feel down, but it is never OK to give up, the people around us do love us, and they do care, and to give up on life will damage and hurt them immeasurably and no they would not be better off without you, believe me, I am not a counsellor, psychologist, or health care professional, but what I am is a fellow human being and here for anyone who needs a chat, a shoulder or a metaphorical kick up the backside, maybe I don't have the answers what worked for me will not work for you, but something will work and you have to keep fighting everyday, after all we need the bad days to appreciate the good ones right?, that goes for anyone.

15 FIN

I really do hope you have enjoyed reading, as much as I have writing this book, it has been a roller coaster of emotions, having to sometimes recall events I had buried deep within myself, I have laughed, cried, and even at times walked away from the keyboard to gather myself and my thoughts before sitting back down with a tear stained face and continue to put the words down as clear and as honest as is possible.

As I said when I started out this is not a "How to do falconry book", I do not deem myself worthy enough to even contemplate such a work, it has been done many times better, by people with the ability to teach, and teach well.

I do however feel responsible to guide anyone reading that wants to learn falconry, and wants to hunt successfully with a hawk of their own, there are a few ways to go about this correctly, find a mentor, someone who lives local to you who is flying birds, and flying them well, most of them don't bite, if they do, simply find someone else, there are plenty of great books out there on Falconry and Hawking, you can either visit the Library, and borrow one, buy the books on-line, I think everyone seriously wanting to take up the sport should get themselves on a course, and you will find no better place to learn than, The International Centre for Birds of Prey, Newent, Glos, It is where I learned, and where the high standards have been maintained over the years, go visit for the day, talk to the staff, and see the birds fly.

What I can tell you is that once hooked, you will be hooked for life, but do please be prepared, you will need to put in time and effort with your bird, seven days a week 365 days a year, even on Christmas Day I spend a couple of hours with my bird and feed him before I sit down to eat my Christmas dinner, but it is also very rewarding, for me there is nothing more pleasurable than a walk round the fields with a well behaved good mannered hawk, don't be like me and fly alone, go out with others and see there birds fly, it can be a social event if you so wish.

RECOMMENDED BOOKS

Falconry and Hawking, Phillip Glasier, ISBN 0 7134 0232 6

A Hawk for the Bush, Jack Mavrogordato, ISBN 85435 082 9

Falconry Care, Captive Breeding and Conservation Jemima Parry-Jones, ISBN 0 7153 8914 9

Veterinary Aspects of Captive Birds of Prey, J E Cooper MRCVS, ISBN 0 904602 04 4

The Sparrowhawk, Ian Newton, ISBN 0 85661 041 0

Ciffy's Tale

www.ingramcontent.com/pod-product-compliance
Lightning Source LLC
Chambersburg PA
CBHW070926290526
45795CB00001B/435